"It comes naturally to avoid what we don't want to feel—especially if we believe we can't heal, that we can't survive the journey into our own pain. Yet I've learned that difficult emotions don't go away—they just go underground. And there they undermine our foundations until finally we must turn our attention their way. In this book you'll find tools for acknowledging complex emotions, bringing them into the light, and welcoming God's healing work. And you'll discover how to move toward a fuller, more hopeful, more compassionate life."

Amy Simpson, author of *Troubled Minds* and *Anxious*

"Few bridges have been built to connect scientific psychological research and practice with spiritual faith communities. Dr. Peace Amadi's book builds this necessary bridge. It offers tangible tools, helping those struggling with mental health difficulties to better understand how to improve their mental health. This is a gift to the Christian community."

Jenny Wang, clinical psychologist and founder of the @asiansformentalhealth community

"In this bracing book, Peace Amadi presents a compelling call for women of faith to examine how intertwined their emotional and spiritual health are—and should be. She offers clear-eyed, accessible advice for determining why our lives fall out of balance, and lays out how to regain clarity and power. Read this book. Better yet, read it and discuss it with other women of faith, and grow together."

Sheryl J. Anderson, television showrunner

"For far too many of us, important conversations around the emotional realities of anxiety, shame, and depression have been glossed over in the name of trusting God. We've all had experiences of receiving well-meaning but ultimately deeply unhelpful advice that equates having faith in God with being free of any emotional struggle. However, in this timely book, Dr. Peace Amadi shows us a path to a different way. With stunning clarity, wisdom, and compassion, she helps us learn how to reframe the important inner work of engaging with God through our emotions, even when it's difficult and confusing. Her profound expertise in psychology, vibrant faith, and warmth come together to create a unique resource that feels like we're somehow sitting in her classroom and at the same time having a heart-to-heart over coffee with a trusted spiritual mentor and friend. You'll be glad that you invested in the spiritual and emotional foundations of your own life with the embodied wisdom and practical tools that this book has to offer."

Tracey Gee, leadership development coach and consultant

"Dr. Peace Amadi recognizes that there is no one-size-fits-all approach to therapy, and her book beautifully navigates different pathways to find solutions to different situations. This is an excellent book for therapists to start learning about different strategies to use within their practices. It is also an excellent read for those who want to live their lives to the fullest by not only understanding their emotions but managing and honoring them as well. You will find yourself and not want to put this book down!"
Melinda Watts, recording artist and influencer

"*Why Do I Feel Like This?* by Peace Amadi helps us navigate the complexity of our emotions. Peace will remind us that it is okay to not be okay."
Heather Thompson Day, associate professor and author of *It's Not Your Turn*

"If your trauma has ever made you feel alienated in your own body, culture, and spiritual community—this book is a salve. It chucks all of the infuriatingly trite but well-meaning advice out the window in favor of practicable, scientifically backed wisdom placed in a spiritual context. Dr. Peace Amadi uses years of clinical experience and teaching to help us befriend and understand our emotions as our body and spirit's best portal for growth. In a comprehensive approach, she breaks down the barriers and stigmas around getting the help we deserve. If you're feeling lost, alone, or overwhelmed, this book is a beautiful road map to healing."
Sarah Montana, TEDx speaker and writer at the Hallmark Channel

WHY DO I FEEL LIKE THIS?

Understand Your Difficult Emotions
and Find Grace to Move Through

PEACE AMADI

An imprint of InterVarsity Press
Downers Grove, Illinois

InterVarsity Press
P.O. Box 1400, Downers Grove, IL 60515-1426
ivpress.com
email@ivpress.com

InterVarsity Press® is the book-publishing division of InterVarsity Christian Fellowship/USA®, a movement of students and faculty active on campus at hundreds of universities, colleges, and schools of nursing in the United States of America, and a member movement of the International Fellowship of Evangelical Students. For information about local and regional activities, visit intervarsity.org.

All Scripture quotations, unless otherwise indicated, are taken from The Holy Bible, New International Version®, NIV®. Copyright © 1973, 1978, 1984, 2011 by Biblica, Inc.™ Used by permission of Zondervan. All rights reserved worldwide. www.zondervan.com. The "NIV" and "New International Version" are trademarks registered in the United States Patent and Trademark Office by Biblica, Inc.™

While any stories in this book are true, some names and identifying information may have been changed to protect the privacy of individuals.

The publisher cannot verify the accuracy or functionality of website URLs used in this book beyond the date of publication.

Cover design and image composite: David Fassett
Interior design: Jeanna Wiggins
Image: untitled photo © Oluseyi Famuyiwa

ISBN 978-0-8308-4772-3 (print)
ISBN 978-0-8308-4773-0 (digital)

Printed in the United States of America ♾

InterVarsity Press is committed to ecological stewardship and to the conservation of natural resources in all our operations. This book was printed using sustainably sourced paper.

Library of Congress Cataloging-in-Publication Data
A catalog record for this book is available from the Library of Congress.

P 28 27 26 25 24 23 22 21 20 19 18 17 16 15 14 13 12 11 10 9 8 7 6 5 4 3 2 1

Y 44 43 42 41 40 39 38 37 36 35 34 33 32 31 30 29 28 27 26 25 24 23 22 21

CONTENTS

Introduction

IT'S WHO WE ARE

I REMEMBER THE FIRST TIME I heard Chris Tomlin's "Good Good Father." I was a first-timer at a small group for a church I'd been newly attending. I had a slight crush on the small group leader, so I was very on time, alert, and ready to receive. But my divided attention quickly became undivided when the group's worship person cued the music and Chris Tomlin's lyrics filled the room:

> *You're a good good Father—it's who you are . . .*
> *And I'm loved by you—it's who I am . . .*[1]

I wasn't new to faith. Quite the veteran, actually, with a résumé full of church leadership positions and some sort of record, I'm sure, for the number of retreats I'd attended. But something about the words made me feel new. Almost like I was seeing the most important thing about God for the first time and hearing his most important thoughts about me. Of all the different things I'd come to believe about myself—via messages from society, media, friends, so-called friends, romantic partners, therapists, teachers, mentors—and all the different labels, descriptions, and names I'd been given, *loved* was the one I wanted to hang on to. *Loved* was decidedly my favorite.

Loved is the most important thing about who we are. But there sure are a lot of other characteristics, aren't there?

For starters, we're needy. We need love, attention, and care. We need connection and community. We need to feel important and significant. We need a sense of meaning for our lives and to be purposeful and creative.

We value and pursue relationships, but we get hurt and grow resentful. We harbor bitterness and unforgiveness. We have a hard time letting things go.

We work hard for what we want but easily grow tired, weary, and discouraged. We let self-doubt take over our minds and rob us of motivation and energy.

Sometimes we're greedy and selfish. Sometimes we're self-centered and ungrateful. And at any given moment, there could be an overflow of negative thoughts and emotions that results in anxiety, insecurity, envy, or depression.

Can you imagine what Chris Tomlin's song would have been like had he tried to include the full reality of who we are? I mean, just picture it:

> You're a good good Father
> It's who you are, it's who you are, it's who you are
> And I'm a needy, greedy, selfish, unforgiving, and ungrateful
> human being struggling with a problem
> It's who I am, it's who I am, it's who I am

Thank God he kept the song simple. Thank God he had the good sense to focus on what God wanted us to hold on to the most.

But even though we are all of the things above and more, it's okay. It's understandable. Because all of it together is what makes us human. Loving, helping, and serving is no more human than hurting, raging, and struggling. We are both beneficiaries and captives of our own humanity. We are all just trying our best.

This is what I would tell you if, like many of my students and clients over the years, you were to burst through my office doors with tear-stained eyes and dwindling hope that you will ever heal from your heartbreak. Or what I would tell you if you were to call me late at night, wondering if you'll ever be able to get right. Or what I would tell you if you lost your zeal for life and let it slip so that you're no longer sure you want to be here.

I would tell you it's okay that you feel this way. I would tell you that you're brave for acknowledging the ugly stuff. I would help you see the strength in your vulnerability. Because I'm all about taking the sting out of things. That sting is the pain of toxic shame—and there's no place for it in your healing.

My hope and prayer for you as you move through these pages is that God would fill you with grace, compassion, and understanding. Perhaps you're great at offering these to others, but I'm asking that you extend them to yourself. If you're struggling with hurt, heartbreak, discouragement, or any of the other emotions covered in this book, I don't wish you to stay where you are. I don't wish you endless weeks of pain and frustration. I wish you health, joy, and freedom. But if there's one thing I've learned as a mental health professional, it's that you can't hate yourself into healing. You have to love yourself right on through it. If God himself, perfect as he is, can love us in the middle of it all, who the heck are we not to?

THE DANGER OF
SPIRITUAL BYPASSING

SOME YEARS AGO, I sat in a pew hoping for a message that would encourage my heart. I was fresh out of a breakup, and as a woman in her thirties, I was starting to experience real doubt that I would ever get my own happy ending. I was also sick and tired of trying to figure dating out. Church, however, was a place I'd always found solace and hope. So I prayed that God would somehow speak to me that morning and crossed my fingers he would.

About three-fourths into the sermon I realized this was *not* going to be the message that encouraged my faith. It was not going to be the message that helped me feel understood. In fact, this was a message I would remember for a long time for how frustrated it made me and so many other women. (Which I found out soon after service.)

See, at this point in the message, the pastor detoured into talking about relationships, and everybody perked up! You could tell he'd struck a chord. He proceeded to talk about the beauty of God's timing, trusting the process, and trusting God at his word. All stuff I'd heard before, but a word doesn't have to be new to be good.

Then came his final exhortation on the topic. Something to the tune of: "So ladies, you need to stop worrying and start working. If you're not married, it's because you're not ready to be. How do I know that? If you were ready, you would be."

I froze. The rest of my row, mostly women, froze also. I could feel us collectively saying, *What did he just say?*

Being a church girl my whole life, I was used to disagreeing with pastors in the pulpit. It happens. In fact, if you told me that you agreed with every single thing your spiritual leader said, I'd be worried that you're not doing enough thinking on your own. I was used to letting things I disagreed with roll off my back and taking from the message only what I felt God really wanted me to hear. I was also used to hard words. Words that pierced through sin in a way you just knew would change you.

But these words weren't hard. They were antagonistic. Because from that position of power and influence came a message that dismissed and invalidated the reality of so many.

It invalidated the challenges of dating in our current culture. A culture where surface, transactional, what-can-I-get-from-you relationships seem to be the norm.

It invalidated the challenges of dating while trying to remain abstinent, which significantly limits your options because many just don't share that value.

It invalidated the real worries of women past their twenties, who confront all kinds of discouraging messages about their ability to find love and start families.

It invalidated the work, and prayers, that grown women have already done in preparation for their marriages, and the weariness and discouragement that comes from years without results. The pastor's words invalidated these realities and more.

What was particularly off-putting, however, were the implications around this idea of readiness. I was a Black professor at a Christian, conservative, predominantly White institution where "ring before spring" was a thing. Every year I witnessed a good number of my senior students get engaged and even married by commencement. I'd get invited to these weddings and happily attend them, and they were always beautiful. But the implication of the pastor's words were that these young, mostly White women were all "ready" for marriage, but the women over thirty I knew, many of them from diverse backgrounds, weren't.

The pastor's statement didn't work for me. The reason for singleness had to be more complicated than just readiness, and instead of taking the time to speak into any number of these realities (which, granted, was a big task), the pastor met our woes with over-spiritualized, trite, hurtful words. I'd gone to church looking for hope and encouragement. I left church feeling emotionally dismissed, deflated, and misunderstood.

THE ANTIWORK OF SPIRITUAL BYPASSING

Do you have a similar story? Have you ever reached out to a fellow believer during a personal challenge or looked to a spiritual leader for counsel and heard some version of the following?

- Just pray about it.
- Let go and let God.
- Just forgive.
- Be strong in the Lord.
- Just have faith.
- There's a reason for everything.
- Just don't worry about it.
- You have so much to be grateful for.
- If you were supposed to have it, you would have it.

If you have, let me tell you now, you have been spiritually bypassed.[1]

Spiritual bypassing is a term coined by psychotherapist and author John Welwood, who used it to describe when we, or other people, use spiritual ideas to belittle our needs, feelings, or personal challenges or to sidestep deep, necessary emotional work. It's when we dole out Christian platitudes and expect the recipient of these easier-said-than-done words to bounce right back into contentment and happiness. It's the equivalent of slapping a fresh cut with a bandage and hoping that any signs of infection will resolve without additional effort. We, and our emotions, deserve better.

It's not that these words of encouragement don't have truth to them. They do, to a degree. The problem is that these words typically come with some sort of expectation that the person experiencing emotional pain or discomfort can just snap out of it. This expectation can lead to a sort of spiritual gaslighting where the reality and gravity of someone's pain is met with a subtle message that says if you *really* walked with God, or if you *really* had enough faith, you wouldn't be feeling this way. Again, we deserve better.

For the record, it is absolutely God's desire that we hold on to faith during our personal crises and challenges. It is absolutely his desire that we pursue and practice love, joy, peace, patience, and all the other fruits of the Spirit. But we are not robots. There's no switch we can turn on to make us automatically become the loftiest version of ourselves. We are complex and complicated. We deal daily with our imperfection and brokenness. We are a work in progress, and God knows this. There would be no need for him in our lives if that wasn't the case.

As for the body of Christ, we need to learn to better embrace our pain. We need to give up our need to have all the answers and instead embrace humility and unknowing. We can't truly enter each other's pain without the ability to hold complexities and discomfort. And without these things, we can't create the kind of community that leads to true healing. We should certainly continue to offer loving words of encouragement, but we must respect the purpose of our emotions and understand that real change, growth, and a deepening of faith take time.

WHAT EXACTLY ARE EMOTIONS?

"Everyone knows what an emotion is, until asked to give a definition. Then, it seems, no one knows." With a touch of humor, researchers Fehr and Russell articulate in their study what emotion theorists have been struggling with for years: emotions are difficult to define![2] Yet the more we learn about our emotions, the better we can appreciate what they offer us. Though there are several broad theories of emotion that differ in some significant ways, one idea that emotion theorists can agree on is that emotions are a multidimensional experience. Here are five components of emotion that work to give us a sense of what we feel from day to day:

Cognitive appraisal. Much like appraisers do for houses or cars, we experience our emotions because we assess the situations that we find ourselves in. We evaluate them. We form meaning out of these events and decide how important each event is to us. If we deem something important, we project what we think needs to be done. Then we decide who's responsible for doing what and form expectations accordingly.

Physiological responses. When we're experiencing an emotion, we may experience increased heart rate, sweating, blushing, nausea, or a number of other physiological changes. If we were to take a picture of what's going in our brain, we would see activation in certain areas.

Expressive behavior. The expressions on our face change as we experience different emotions. The tone and the inflection of our voice may change. The way we use touch may shift. Our nonverbals often express our emotions more honestly than our words.

Subjective experience. What emotions feel like to us is our subjective experience of them. Usually this is identified by the words we use to describe them. We'll take our appraisals, feel out the changes happening in our body, and describe our emotions with feeling words—*happy, sad, mad, glad, anxious,* etc. Being able to name what your emotions feel like is an important first step in being able to work through them.

Action tendencies. Finally, our emotions motivate us to act in certain ways. Happiness inspires us to show gratitude. Sadness can lead us to want to sleep. Anger on behalf of others can lead us to act in ways that will restore justice and equality. Guilt may motivate us to make amends.

Emotions are judgments. According to cognitive appraisal theorists, emotions can also be understood as judgments. To paraphrase the theory, emotions are judgments about the extent to which a situation has met your goals. Happiness is what we experience when our goals are met. We apply for the job and we get it. We search for love and we find it. We pray for a family member's healing and we witness it. We ask God for a financial breakthrough and a check comes in the mail. You get the picture. In contrast, sadness is an emotion we're likely to feel if our goals aren't satisfied. Anger, frustration, discouragement, and envy are emotions that may emerge as well. Emotions bring clarity about what we truly need and want.

Emotions as energy. It can also be helpful to think about our emotions as a kind of energy—psychological energy, if you will, that flows throughout our body when something triggers it. This idea is what motivates many therapists to ask their clients: "Where do you feel this anger in your body?" "Where do you feel your sadness or anxiety?" Questions like these help us grow more aware of how we carry our emotions—in our stomach, neck, back, or legs—and how often we experience them.

Sometimes we feel an expansion of this energy, like when we experience joy, excitement, or love. This energy causes us to feel light on our feet, free of burden, and filled with all things good. Other times we feel a contraction of this energy, such as when we experience sadness, fear, or hurt. Consequently, we feel heavy, lethargic, and as though something is weighing us down. That something is negative energy, and when it's moving through our body, it's hard to miss.

Recall what you've learned about energy, perhaps from a past physics course. Energy cannot be created or destroyed; it can only be transferred or transformed. This is the law of the conservation of energy, and we can apply it to our understanding of the way emotions work.

What happens to your anger when you don't have an outlet to release it? What happens in your relationships when you keep swallowing your frustration? Nothing good.

That's because feelings don't evaporate; they accumulate. Unattended to, they grow into something more. What we resist persists. Unexpressed negative feelings get stored in our minds and bodies only to later manifest in rage, resentment, broken relationships, chronic health issues, anxiety-boosting avoidance, passive aggressiveness, and undesired changes in personality. Our feelings will move throughout our body until we do something with them.

Emotions connect us to each other and ourselves. Imagine for a second what life would be without emotions.

Without feelings of attraction, we couldn't be drawn to the people who are supposed to be in our lives. Without love, we would have no reason to commit to each other, knit our lives together, or build families. Without empathy, we couldn't feel for one another, which is exactly what inspires us to help, support, and be there for each other when we need it. Without hurt and anger, we couldn't honor our needs, expectations, or our sense of personal boundaries. Emotions help us cultivate healthy, long-lasting relationships.

Emotions reflect God in us. *I'm so emotional!* How many times have you said this to yourself, perhaps out of frustration or annoyance because it felt like it was something you couldn't change or control? I have thought this many times and have struggled to see it as a good thing.

But a few years ago, I had a revelation about my own emotionality. I'd been encouraged to do a study on God's emotions, and on one quiet morning, it occurred to me: *Wow, God is so emotional too!*

Scripture is replete with stories of God feeling and expressing those feelings. We especially see these emotions in the stories of Jesus. To name a few instances, the Bible tells us that:

- Jesus lamented over Israel's rejection (Matthew 27:46).

- Jesus felt anger and indignation at the people in the temple and threw them out (Matthew 21:12).

- Jesus was overcome with feeling and wept for Lazarus (John 11:34-35).

- Jesus felt, but withstood, the strength of temptation (Hebrews 4:15).

- Jesus felt compassion for the crowds of people who seemed spiritually lost (Matthew 9:36) and also for people who were tired and hungry (Matthew 15:32).

- Jesus felt love for a stranger who asked him a question about life (Mark 10:21).

- Jesus felt forsaken (Matthew 27:46).

Scripture is clear. God has a robust emotional life. Of course, he responds to these feelings without sin. He doesn't turn to debauchery to cope with anger or intense sadness. He doesn't harm those who disappoint him. He doesn't give in to the enemy's temptation. But he feels. Just like us.

Genesis 1:26 says: "Then God said, 'Let us make mankind in our image, in our likeness.'" The emotions we have are a reflection of God in us. We feel because he feels. It's in our spiritual DNA. Unlike God, we sometimes let our emotions lead us into sin and darkness, but our emotions are normal and natural for us just as they are normal and natural for our God.

Emotions draw us back to God. Perhaps my favorite thing about our emotions is how they draw us back to God. Happiness gives us reason to praise him. Hurt, anger, and distress give us reason to seek him. Confusion causes us to seek his counsel. In discouragement and weariness we look for his encouragement and hope. In loneliness, we look for his companionship. In grief and sorrow, we're in desperate need of his comfort. Our emotions are often a catalyst for communion with God.

When we spiritually bypass our emotions, we lose far more than we gain. Even our uncomfortable emotions have much to teach us about ourselves, our world, and our God. These emotions often create pathways for our healing; they work as a guide to what God ultimately wants for us. What a gift.

DEALING, HEALING, AND MOVING THROUGH

Now, let's be honest. The gift of emotions doesn't make dealing with the uncomfortable ones any easier. It doesn't take away from the fact that hurt, anger, envy, anxiety, depression and other unwanted emotions can break us down and take over our lives and relationships.

These emotions always require that we deal with them—that we feel them, release them, and move them along when we can. Other times, they require that we do more than just deal and actually *heal*. Such is the case when you realize that your emotions cut much deeper and may represent unresolved issues, traumas, or spiritual bondages in your life. What your uncomfortable emotions require will vary by person, situation, and story.

When healing is required, I find it's helpful to have a clear understanding of what it looks like. What's the end goal? What can you expect in your healing journey?

In my work I use a six-part framework, born out of my research and experiences, to describe this healing.

Healing is freedom. Like healing of the body, emotional healing is freedom from what caused you pain. As you heal, there will likely be less and less emotional charge when you think or talk about the event that affected you. You may get to a point where you even take pride in your "scars." Your pain may take on new meaning and the "symptoms" (anger, anxiety, shame, etc.) that once accompanied it will dissipate or altogether disappear.

Healing is personal control and agency. In healing, there is a sense that you are no longer bound by your wounds or trapped by your memories. Your actions are no longer driven by pain or revenge. You move independently and have power to make new choices. You create new realities for your life.

Healing is wholeness. When healing, you start to believe and feel that you are complete within yourself. Nothing feels broken, nothing feels like it's missing. This is the true definition of shalom, by the way. You are able to find your peace.

Healing is harmony. You are not one person in one situation and another person in a different situation. You are wholly yourself everywhere. There is no part of you that hides or cowers in shame or fear of rejection. You have accepted every part of you. Everything now works together in sync. There is inner harmony.

Healing is wholehearted living. With self-understanding, self-love, and self-compassion, and with newfound freedom, wholeness, agency, and inner harmony, every part of you lives fully. You are present, grateful, and engaged in your life. You leave nothing on the table. There is no fear.

Healing is a process. The nature of healing is cyclical. Imagine climbing up a mountain. It's impossible to walk straight up. To get to the top, you must go around and around it again but realize that with each loop, you are getting farther up. Emotional healing works the same way. On the journey, you may feel frustrated that a feeling you thought was gone forever returns. You may feel scared that though your childhood trauma happened so long ago, you're still triggered by things here and there. There will be seasons of peace, interjected by seasons of anxiety. But this is the nature of healing. True healing is a lifelong journey. When old stuff comes back up, reject the idea that you're slacking or falling back. You're simply moving up that mountain. You're getting another opportunity to see God do work in you.

Whenever you're ready to deal with or heal from your emotions, whether through this book or some other time, commit to doing the work. Reject the temptation to bypass your emotions or the pressure to let others do that to you. Reject the temptation to avoid, suppress, or pretend that your hurt, trauma, sadness, depression, and grief aren't there. Realize there is only one way to get to the other side of your difficult emotions: moving through.

UNCOVERING OUR CORE BELIEFS

*All people cross the line from childhood
to adulthood with a secondhand opinion of who they are.
Without any questioning, we take as truth whatever our parents
and other influentials have said about us during our childhood,
whether these messages are communicated
verbally, physically, or silently.*

HEYWARD EWART

*What matters is not the idea a man holds, but
the depth at which he holds it.*

EZRA POUND

*Do not conform to the pattern of this world, but be
transformed by the renewing of your mind.*

ROMANS 12:2

We are lovable.

MELODY BEATTIE

CHASTA'S STORY
I KEPT ON ATTRACTING UNAVAILABLE MEN

I was forty, single, and very ready to mingle, but also depressed. I'd spent the last few years falling for different guys in my life, and they were all unavailable.

First there was Jordan. We'd flirted at work for months before he asked me out. He was biracial—Black and Mexican—but for some reason, he preferred not to date Black women. Apparently I was "different." One night, he shared that he had a complicated relationship with his Black mother and felt there were still unresolved issues due to her abusive tendencies growing up. This just drew me in more. I think on some level I felt I could fix him. But soon after this conversation, he ghosted. Never heard from him again. Thankfully I'd already moved on. To Cory.

Cory messaged me one night on Instagram, telling me everything I could ever want to hear. He spoke decisively, which was really attractive to me, and soon we were talking about marriage and family. But Cory had an ex he'd just broken up with and "she just wouldn't leave [him] alone." I was concerned, but I just made him promise to cut off communication with her, and he said he would. One day we got into an argument, and I told him I needed space for a few days. He gave me space all right, right from the arms of his ex, who he ran back to. Come to find out, he had never cut her off. He just needed to see what else was out there.

Then there was Brady. Brady and I met at a business meeting, and there was an instant connection. I got ahead of myself and started planning our next few dates in my head, only for him to rudely interrupt my fantasy with talk about a girlfriend. Huh? Then why have we been sitting here sharing our souls for hours? I was crushed. I drove home and swore to never talk with him again. That all changed when he called me later in the week and admitted he'd been unhappy in his relationship. Cue our intense emotional affair full of late-night FaceTimes and some overnight dates. After a few months, he broke up with her and officially asked to be with me. I was happy, but I was also unsure. Was this right?

Could he really be over her? Was he really ready to start a relationship with me? I didn't think so, but I ignored my gut. Then, surprising no one, we started dating and crashed and burned. About a month or so later, I got an update on Facebook: Brady was engaged. To his ex, of course.

THOUGHTS AND BELIEFS

This is a book about tough emotions. However, we would be remiss to jump in and start talking about understanding and overcoming these emotions, or the unproductive behaviors that ensue, without first acknowledging the role of our thoughts in sustaining them.

In the years that I practiced psychotherapy, teaching the relationship between thoughts, feelings, and behaviors was key to my clients' healing journey. This relationship is the main focus of cognitive behavioral therapy (CBT), a popular psychotherapy approach to treating various mental health issues.

CBT succinctly depicts the relationship between thoughts, feelings, and behaviors by using what's commonly referred to as the cognitive triangle. The idea is simple: our thoughts affect our feelings, our feelings affect our behaviors, and our behaviors affect and further reinforce our thoughts. As an example, think about a mother who thinks to herself, *I'm failing as a parent.* This thought will likely cause

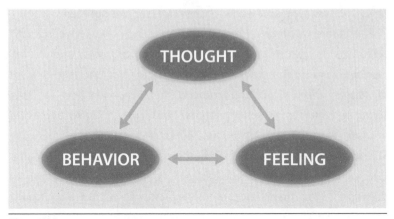

Figure 2.1

her to feel negative feelings—like sadness and guilt—which may cause her to oversleep often and emotionally disengage. A mother who oversleeps and disengages will likely end up missing important parenting opportunities like picking up her child from school or comforting her child in distress. This in turn will have a negative effect on the child, lead to fall out, and only serve to confirm the mother's idea that she is failing as a parent. See the problem?

Now notice the direction of the arrows in the cognitive triangle. It is overly simplistic to believe that the relationship between thoughts, feelings, and behaviors are always one-directional. In real life, thoughts influence feelings, but feelings can also influence thoughts. Feelings influence behaviors, but behaviors can also influence feelings. CBT doesn't negate the different ways our feelings are affected, but it does suggest thoughts are the best starting place for healing mental and emotional concerns.

NOT ALL THOUGHTS ARE CREATED EQUAL

You and I have thousands of thoughts going through our heads a day. In fact, according to the Laboratory of NeuroImaging at USC, we produce about 48.6 thoughts per minute.[1] That sums up to about 70,000 thoughts per day. That's a whole lot of thinking!

But not all thoughts are created equal. Many of these thoughts are useless, unimportant ideas that pass through our minds automatically and with great speed. You typically don't even notice they are there until you're trying to do something else—read, study, focus on a lecture, and so on—and realize there's quite a bit of mental noise competing for your attention. These passing thoughts don't matter much to our well-being.

Then there are the thoughts that do matter. Thoughts like the example used earlier—*I'm failing as a parent*—that are ideas we entertain about our lives and ourselves. These ideas are powerful enough to affect our feelings and actions and are relatively easy to identify once we give ourselves the time and space.

Finally, there are our beliefs. The distinction between thoughts and beliefs isn't one that every mental health professional will make, but it's one I've found important for healing—both my clients' and my own. Beliefs are also thoughts, but they can be far more insidious.

Here's a metaphor I use to help distinguish the two. Imagine having an open house party. By the nature of the event, you have guests in your home that you know very well, guests you consider acquaintances, and guests you've never met. When your best friends walk into the house, you let them go wherever they want. They have free rein in your home. You trust them. With the acquaintances, you'll be a bit more cautious and require that they stay in the common party room. If they cross any boundaries, you'll offer a friendly warning first, and if need be, ask them to leave. With strangers, you'll exercise even greater caution and watch them like a hawk. Any problems with them at all and they'll be let out quicker than they got in.

Thoughts are like the strangers and acquaintances we let in. We entertain them, but we can dismiss them if they start to affect us negatively. Sometimes it takes some effort, but typically we can get the job done. Beliefs, however, are like those best friends. We've so fully accepted them into our lives that even if they're up to no good, we may have a hard time seeing it.

CORE BELIEFS, DEFINED

Our hurt, anger, anxiety, and discouragement are often the result of a negative thought life. But sometimes, these emotional experiences are rooted in something deeper. Sometimes, they are the result of a deep set of personal beliefs about ourselves, other people, and the world. These beliefs are our core beliefs. Like the best friends at the house party, they're difficult to let go of.

Core beliefs reflect how worthy we think we are. They reflect how lovable, significant, and capable we think we are. Core beliefs reflect what we expect from people. Will they show up for us? Will they be there when we need them? Will they stay? Core beliefs reflect what we believe the world has to offer. For some, the world feels generous and plentiful. For others, the world feels scarce and dim. Whatever the case, core beliefs impact every part of our lives. Though they were once just thoughts we entertained, our life experiences have made them feel like personal truths.

THE RISE OF CORE BELIEFS

Once upon a time, as a child, you had a thought. You developed this thought about something you went through: a hard day at school, a problem with a parent, a talk with your teacher, an embarrassing experience with peers. Then, because of the way we are all wired, you formed a thought that would help you make sense of the situation or at the very least come to a conclusion in order to figure out a way to move on. Unfortunately, many of these thoughts didn't work in your favor. They were negative, limiting, and self-deprecating:

- *I'm being picked on, I don't fit in.*

- *My dad is upset with me again, I can never do things right.*

- *My teacher is disappointed, I'm not as smart as everyone else.*

- *My friends don't want to be friends anymore, I'm a nobody.*

Some of these thoughts came directly from you. Some of these thoughts were planted by the words of someone else. Regardless, the thoughts swam around in your head until one of two things happened: (1) you or someone you trusted intervened and decisively found a more helpful way for you to think about the situation. Or (2) you did not have the opportunity to challenge these negative ideas and in fact probably found yourself in situations later that seemed to confirm these ideas again and again. Then, with all this evidence stacked against you, you would come to a hard conclusion. This thought is your *truth*.

MY INTERNALIZED BULLY

I remember when I first became aware of some of my own core beliefs. I had noticed some unproductive patterns in my work and relationships, so I sought out a therapist to help me understand them. As expected, we spent some time diving into my childhood, which unfortunately included years of being bullied by different kids at school. I knew these experiences had influenced me somewhat, but I hadn't realized the gravity of that influence. The bullies of my childhood weren't just sore memories of the past. I'd internalized their voices.

You can't sit here. You don't fit. Something is wrong with you. Everything you do is wrong. You don't belong. These were the kinds of messages that drove some of the unwanted patterns in my life. These were the voices of those bullies.

I have to admit that when I first realized this, I felt a little bit of shame. I couldn't believe that common childhood bullying could have such an effect on me. "This is lame!" I would say to my therapist. "It's not like I was abused or abandoned!" I struggled to accept that my personal experiences were significant enough to cause any kind of real emotional damage. This, of course, was also the result of these beliefs. If something was wrong with me, if everything I did was wrong, my feelings had to be wrong too. My feelings about the past were just another case of me being "too sensitive," and I needed to get over it.

But time in therapy and a decade's worth of research showing the deep, enduring impact of verbal abuse from peers helped me find the self-compassion and grace to accept that this was my story. And it was a valid one.

The first thing I needed to do was stop blaming my sensitivity. Sure, I had always been a sensitive kid. I'd always felt things more deeply, intensely, and for a longer period of time than most people around me. As an adult, I still do. But my sensitivity wasn't the problem here. It wasn't a liability as I'd allowed myself to believe. My sensitivity only meant that things really mattered to me and that I needed tools to work with it. "The problem in our world isn't too much sensitivity, it's too little," my therapist would say to me, and she would challenge me to see it as my gift.

Looking back on her words, I believe they were God speaking his own words of love and acceptance through her. I believe God was trying to show me that the soft parts of me reflected the soft parts of him. This moment felt like it was an invitation to welcome my emotions as an opportunity to connect more intimately with him. I'm thankful for how that moment has changed my life and work.

The second thing I needed to do was acknowledge that the internalized voices were driving patterns of paralyzing perfectionism, a need to be in control, and deep fears of failure that stood in the way of some of the things I wanted most. I would mentally play out scenarios of taking new steps and trying new things and immediately hear mocking laughter and humiliating remarks in my head. I was extremely self-conscious because growing up I had to be. Deep down I believed the bullying wasn't the fault of the bullies; it was mine. If I could finally do everything right, it would stop. If I kept doing everything right, it would never happen again.

These beliefs formed at an early time in life but stayed with me. Becoming aware of them was my first step to freedom and healing.

THE LARGE UNSEEN

Perhaps the most nefarious thing about our core beliefs is that they are unconscious. We are not immediately aware of the beliefs we hold about ourselves and our world, but that doesn't stop these beliefs from affecting our lives.

Our mind can be divided into two parts: the conscious and the unconscious. Our conscious mind contains the needs, wants, thoughts, feelings, fears, and memories that we are aware of. For example, if I were to ask you what you are needing or wanting right now, you would be able to tell me. What you'd say would come from your conscious mind.

In contrast, our unconscious mind contains the stuff that we are not currently aware of. These are the needs, wants, thoughts, feelings, fears, and memories that we formed in childhood that have fallen and stayed beneath the surface of our awareness as adults. This happens when things are too emotionally overwhelming to deal with head on, or there just isn't time, space, or know-how to do so. The self is protective by nature and rises to our defense when we are being hurt. This is where the term "defense mechanisms" comes from. Repression (blocking out thoughts and feelings to the point of forgetting), displacement (redirecting and taking out feelings on the wrong person, usually a safer target), and denial (refusal to accept reality) are some of the most commonly used defense mechanisms.

The thing is, just because these thoughts, feelings, and fears fell away from conscious awareness doesn't mean they stopped affecting us. It's quite the contrary. Our unconscious mind has been influencing our behavior this entire time. In fact, the unconscious mind is thought to be an even more powerful determinant of behavior than our conscious one.

Have you ever had a dream that shocked you? Or hinted that you were deeply worried about something you didn't even realize was bothering you? Or have you ever had an "I can't believe I just said that out loud" moment and wished you could take things back? Or have you ever teared up all of a sudden during a conversation and found yourself surprised by your level of emotion? If you have, know that these are examples of your unconscious mind trying to express itself and tell you something important. Dreams, slips of the tongue, and strong, unexpected emotion are just a few of the ways our unconscious mind tries to remind us that it's holding everything we dream of and desire. It's holding our unresolved needs and beliefs. It's holding our wishes and urges, no matter how silly or childlike. It's holding the pains of our childhood and memories.

A BIBLICAL CASE FOR THE UNCONSCIOUS?

If you're wondering whether the Bible supports the psychological idea of the unconscious, then good. As a believer myself, I consider all my ideas against what I know of Scripture, and I encourage you to do the same. That being said, we can be certain about the emphasis God puts on our mind. The Word is quite clear on the importance of tending to our thoughts and minds.

- Romans 12:2 exhorts us to "be transformed by the renewing of your mind."

- Philippians 4:8, one of my all-time favorites, tells us to focus our minds on things that are true, noble, right, pure, lovely, admirable, excellent, or praiseworthy.

- Second Corinthians 10:5 says with the Holy Spirit's help we can "demolish arguments" and "take captive" the thoughts that go against our knowledge of God, which at the end of the day creates our knowledge of self.

- Colossians 3:2 encourages us to "set [our] minds on things above, not on earthly things."

But do any of these make a case for the unconscious part of our minds?

A pastor, John, once did an interview that looked at this question. In a conversation about the way we engage Scripture, he was asked by a listener: "Must we come away from our Bible reading with a life principle or a specific point of application every time?" To which John had much to say:

> I feel pretty strongly about this. The answer is no. And here is why I feel strongly about it. I would say maybe 99 percent of our lives is lived without immediate reflection upon a life principle. Rather, we just act. If you think about your day, there are maybe a hundred big decisions you make in a day. And by "big" I just mean "conscious." But right now, I am just talking to you. I am

just choosing words. Before every word, I am not stopping and saying, "Now, what principle is going to govern this word, and what principle is going to govern this sentence? They are just kind of tumbling out of me right now. That's scary, right? Where did they come from? . . . Most of our lives are lived spontaneously. Most of our lives are not lived after ten seconds of reflection on a biblical principle. They come from being a kind of person. . . . I am not opposed to principles. Good night, I write books in which I am trying to do things so they are helpful to meditate on. But that is the key: meditating on truth shapes the soul. We become what we behold.

At this point, the interviewer interjects and suggests that John may be actually speaking about the influence of our unconscious on our behavior. The interviewer then asks: "Pastor John, do you think it is appropriate to talk about the subconscious here?" To which John responded:

Yes. That is basically what I was trying to say, that most of our life is lived from resources that are not presently reflected on in our mind. Our words are coming from inside—"What comes out of the mouth proceeds from the heart, and this defiles a person" (Matthew 15:18). And most of that heart is unconscious or subconscious and that is shaped day by day by what we are taking in. It is shaped by what we do with our eyes on the computer, and it is especially shaped by what we do with our Bibles and our prayer. Whenever I pray, I am pleading with God, "Work down deeper than I can get in my reading right now. Take your scalpel, and don't just deal with the sins I am aware of: go be a surgeon."[2]

I appreciate the pastor's words here. More significantly, his inspired revelations and the science of the mind line up. Our lives are lived from the inside out. The words we speak, emotions we feel, attractions we harness, and choices we make are not thought out at every point and turn. They are spontaneous productions of whatever is going on deep down in our core. Our core beliefs are a central part of that core.

The Scripture referenced here—Matthew 15:18—raises an important question. When the verse says "But the things that come out of a person's mouth come from the heart," the original Greek word for "heart" here is *kardia*. Interestingly, *kardia* is referenced over eight hundred other times in Scripture, but none of those references refer to the physical organ we each carry. Instead, the word *kardia* is defined as the "center and seat of life," "the center and seat of will and character," and the "fountain and seat of thoughts, passions, desires, appetites, affections, purposes, endeavors."[3]

Could "heart" be Scripture's word for the psychologist's unconscious mind? Could the psychologist's unconscious mind be our best stab at defining what Scripture refers to as heart? I will leave this for you to ponder and decide. But my sense is that there is something true here.

WHAT HAVE YOU ACCEPTED AS TRUE?

Let's return to Chasta's story from the top of this chapter:

Finally, there was Timothy. Timothy was married. Separated, but married. He was married when I met him, married when I fell for him, married through our secret relationship, and married after I finally let him go. It wasn't until I worked with a therapist that I learned that my tendency to attract unavailable men wasn't just a matter of being unlucky. It was a problem with my beliefs. For one, I knew that at some level I believed I was just too hard to love. Too difficult. I didn't really believe anybody could love me wholeheartedly. So when someone offered me an inferior version of it, I took it. When someone loved me just a little bit, I was all in. Real love felt so scarce to me. It felt like it was only readily available to the most beautiful and deserving. I didn't believe I was either. I had to take what I could get.

The first step in Chasta's healing journey required identifying her problematic core beliefs. It required looking at the patterns in her life and uncovering what bubbled beneath the surface. It required challenging what she's always believed to be true. This is a call for each of us. What ideas about yourself have you come to accept as true?

UNCOVERING YOUR CORE BELIEFS

Remember that due to their unconscious nature, the deep-seated truths operating in our lives aren't terribly obvious. Thankfully, our lives can offer some clues. Core beliefs contribute to many of our day-to-day emotional experiences. They play a role in those experiences becoming real, persistent struggles. They influence our relationship patterns. They motivate our life decisions.

You can work to uncover your core beliefs by examining the emotions, patterns, and choices that characterize your days. To this aim, here are some questions you can use to begin the process. Treat it like a self-interview, and be as honest with yourself as you can.

- What feelings have been coming up for me lately?
- What things do people do to me or tell me that I find most hurtful?
- What "little things" have been making me irritated or angry?
- What issues keep coming up either personally or relationally?
- What patterns have I been noticing in my life or relationships?
- What choices do I regret but keep on repeating?

For the feeling questions in particular, try following up your answers with the questions "Why is this so important?" or "Why is this so bad?"

For example, someone says to you "you're too sensitive," which causes you to go from zero to one hundred on a scale of high negative emotion. Follow-up questioning could look like you asking yourself, *Why is this so bad?*

To which you might respond, *Because it hurts my feelings.*

Follow-up question: *But why?*

Response: *Because it makes me feel like I'm crazy.*

Follow-up question: *Why is that so bad?*

Response: *Because crazy people don't get loved, they get left.*

Follow-up question: *Why is that important?*

Response: *Because the people I love always leave me. I'm always getting abandoned.*

In this case, one of the core beliefs at work could be stated as: "The people I love leave me." Another, less obvious belief could be: "I'm hard to love."

Again, I ask you, what have you accepted as true?

CORE BELIEF CHECKLIST

Another way to try and uncover core beliefs is to see which ones resonate with you. The Core Belief Checklist is a list I've pulled together that identifies some of the most common core beliefs at work in our daily lives. Inspired by my work and some accessible research, the list is organized into eight problem areas in which our core beliefs seem to wade: defectiveness, lovability, belonging, significance, capability, fears about abandonment, fears about support, and fears about safety from harm.

Create space and time to work through the checklist. Read each belief statement slowly and contemplatively. Notice the shifts in your emotions and energy. The ones that may hold true for you will resonate with you. Put a check next to the ones that do. When you're done, pull back and see if you notice any patterns. Do most of your checks fall into one or two categories? Which categories are those?

I encourage you to process this checklist with a trusted friend or counselor who knows you well. It can be hard to see some of these beliefs in ourselves, and an external voice can help with blind spots. One question you can ask them is, "Do you hear me say any of these things about myself?" Be open to what they say.

Table 2.1

THE CORE BELIEF CHECKLIST (Eight Areas of Core Beliefs)	

Defectiveness

- ○ I'm not good enough.
- ○ I can't get anything right.
- ○ I'm inferior to other people.
- ○ I don't measure up.
- ○ I'm useless.
- ○ I'm nothing.
- ○ I'm worthless.
- ○ I'm unattractive.

- ○ I'm ugly.
- ○ I'm always wrong.
- ○ Everything I do is wrong.
- ○ I'm a failure.
- ○ There is something wrong with me.
- ○ There is something missing.
- ○ I am irredeemably flawed.
- ○ I am crazy.

Lovability

- ○ I'm not lovable.
- ○ I'm too difficult to love.
- ○ I'm hard to love.
- ○ I'm unacceptable.
- ○ I'm not wanted.

- ○ I'm uninteresting.
- ○ Nobody loves me.
- ○ Nobody wants me.
- ○ I'm bound to be rejected.
- ○ Nobody could really ever love me.

Belonging

- ○ I don't belong.
- ○ I don't fit in.
- ○ I don't fit in anywhere.
- ○ I'm always left out.
- ○ I'm unwelcome.
- ○ I'm an outsider.

- ○ I'm different.
- ○ I'm weird.
- ○ I'm always alone.
- ○ No one understands me.
- ○ I'm abnormal.

Significance

- ○ I don't matter.
- ○ I'm unimportant.
- ○ I'm not as good as other people.
- ○ I'm only worthwhile if I'm doing something special.
- ○ I'm only worthwhile if I'm helping someone.
- ○ I am insignificant.
- ○ If I don't excel, I am inferior.
- ○ If I don't excel, I am a failure.

- ○ If people don't respect me, they should be punished.
- ○ If people don't pay attention to me, I can't stand it.
- ○ I deserve more attention and praise.
- ○ People should go out of their way for me.
- ○ I am invisible.

Table 2.1 (continued)

Capability

- I am helpless.
- I have no power.
- I am weak.
- I am trapped.
- There's no way out.
- I am needy.
- I am ineffective.
- I am unsuccessful.
- I can't do it.
- I can't change.
- I can't handle anything.
- I finish last.
- I always lose.
- I can't stand up for myself.
- I can't say no.

Fears About Abandonment

- People I love will leave me.
- If I love someone, they will leave me.
- If I assert myself, people will leave me.
- If I say what I feel, people will leave me.
- If I am too strong, people will leave me.
- I am uninteresting.
- I am too sensitive.
- I am too much.
- Something is missing in me.
- People lose interest in me.
- I can't hang on to anybody.
- I'm bound to be rejected.
- I'm bound to be abandoned.
- People leave and don't come back.

Fears About Support

- I don't need to ask for help.
- If I ask for help, I'll be disappointed.
- I have to do everything myself.
- I have to do everything perfectly.
- If I don't do it, no one will.
- I'm responsible for everything.
- I can't trust anyone.
- I can't rely on anyone.
- If I trust, I'll be disappointed (and I won't survive it).
- If I trust people, they may hurt me (and I won't survive it).
- People don't show up for me.
- People can't be trusted.
- People will betray me.

Fears About Safety from Harm

- I am not safe.
- My heart always gets broken.
- People will hurt me.
- People will be cruel to me.
- People will make fun of me.
- If I express myself, terrible things will happen.
- I always get hurt.

Keep in mind that uncovering core beliefs isn't a quick and easy process. It's a subtle, dynamic process that takes time. While some of your core beliefs may have jumped out at you now, there will be others that will later surprise you. Others that won't be revealed to you until a different season, situation, or relationship. Be open to the spontaneous discovery of your core beliefs.

CHANGING YOUR CORE BELIEFS

Changing your core beliefs requires action. Fortunately, awareness of your beliefs can help clarify the actions you need to take. These actions create what psychologists call a "corrective experience." This is an experience where new actions and interactions create a new result. The new experience "corrects" the old one.

For example, in Chasta's case, a new action would be taking the time to learn more about the men she's attracted to and being vigilant about engaging strictly with the ones who prove to be fully present and emotionally available. Though this may take more time and energy, and though it may bring the feelings of discomfort that often come with unfamiliar territory, the investment would be well worth it. Having a successful dating experience with an emotionally available man would likely be the corrective experience she needs to believe that she is worthy of someone's whole heart.

THE QUESTION OF POSITIVE AFFIRMATIONS

When you seek out self-help on changing your thoughts and beliefs, you'll find a ton of stuff on positive self-affirmations and positive self-talk. This is for good reason, as saying positive things about and to yourself has proven to be a helpful method for combating harsh internal dialogue and improving negative thoughts.

However, positive words don't always lead to the change that we seek, and if they do, they typically work at the level of our thoughts. If your patterns are rooted in previously formed core beliefs, you'll likely need something more. Beliefs don't change on account of good words. Beliefs need to be altered at the level they were created. *New beliefs require new experiences.*

As we dive into the next eight chapters, remember to consider the full context of where your emotions live. It isn't just our brains, bodies, and life experiences that give power to our negative emotions; it's our core beliefs as well.

TRAUMA

Our Need to Tell Our Story

Jesus asked the boy's father, "How long has he been like this?"
"From childhood," he answered.

MARK 9:21

Trauma is personal. It does not disappear if it is not validated.
When it is ignored or invalidated the silent screams continue
internally, heard only by the one held captive.
When someone enters the pain and hears
the screams, healing can begin.

DANIELLE BERNOCK

Unlike other forms of psychological disorders,
the core issue in trauma is reality.

BESSEL A. VAN DER KOLK

Only when we are brave enough to explore the darkness
will we discover the infinite powers of our light.

BRENÉ BROWN

AUDREY'S STORY
MY UNCLE ABUSED ME WHEN I WAS FIVE

When I was five years old, I was taken from my parents due to their drug addiction and placed in the care of my aunt and uncle. But just weeks after I moved into my new home, my uncle began to sexually abuse me. Eventually, he was exposed, but this created tension in the family. My aunt took out her frustration by physically abusing me and my two younger sisters. This lasted my entire childhood. The only thing I knew to do was survive. As a child, you see how other families are portrayed. You're taught in school that sexual abuse is wrong. You learn that parents aren't supposed to beat their children. But when that's your life, you just think, "Well, maybe it's just different for me." You also just don't want to think about the fact that the people who are supposed to raise and love you are the ones hurting you. You just don't want to think about it.

It wasn't until my second year of college that I saw any justice. I couldn't live the lie that everything was fine anymore, so I finally went to the authorities to save both myself and my sisters. This gave me the strength to begin my journey of healing and to finally look at how the abuse had impacted me. Being at a Christian university, one of the first things I had to confront were my feelings toward God. I didn't blame God. I understood we all had free will, and people made their own choices to hurt others. But it was still hard. There were times when I cried out to God and felt absolutely nothing. I would just sit there. God's silence messes with you a bit. You feel lonely and abandoned.

But I also had to look at my people pleasing. I remember that with my aunt and uncle, I always tried to do everything I could to feel accepted by them. I guess I hoped that if I was good enough, all the hurting would stop. It's still important to me that people think highly of me. I think it is for everyone, but I think I needed it even more. My now husband has helped a lot with that though. He's shown me so much love and respect for just being me. It makes me emotional when I think about it. Having someone who can support you totally and completely is really helpful.

Today, I'm a mother to a two-month-old baby girl. I do worry at times about being a good mother to her, but I know that fear comes from my past. She is my world, and I know I will do everything I can to protect her from harm. She is also my reminder that life is a miracle. Her life and, honestly, my life too. This is why one of my main goals in life is to help those who struggle with their dark pasts while also raising kind souls who will help build a less painful world in the future.

BRITISH'S STORY
MY BROTHER TOOK HIS OWN LIFE

In January of 2017, my brother took his life. I found out coming home from the grocery store. I had just parked my car in front of my apartment entrance, and not in my normal parking spot, so it would be easier for me to take my groceries up to the second floor. As soon as I parked, I got the call: he'd killed himself. In complete shock, I managed to walk up the stairs, but as soon as I got to the top, I burst out crying. I remember a stranger asked me if I was okay and if I needed help. I don't remember what I said to him. Everything was a blur.

I was all the way on the other side of the country, away from my whole family. I was left with my thoughts, totally alone. I couldn't help but go back and forth in my mind. What could I have done to prevent this from happening? How could I have been a better sister? How come I didn't check on him more often? I felt like a terrible person. I blamed myself. Then the blame turned to guilt. How dare I make this about me? How dare I be selfish and naive? The guilt spiraled into depression and anxiety. Then I got mean. I was a leader at my church during this time, but I was angry. I didn't know how to manage all these feelings, so I turned them on everybody else. It got to the point that no one wanted to be around me, which was fine because I didn't want to be around them. I ignored my responsibilities. I ignored the messages my pastors brought forth. I lost my faith.

It wasn't until the end of that year that I'd had enough. I allowed myself to become vulnerable enough to receive help. For me, that came

*in the form of gracious pastors who supported me, prayed for me, and
helped me see God more clearly. Two years later, I'm full of faith but still
have moments of depression and anxiety. Instead of ignoring it, though,
I pray about it and reach out for help. I know my trauma won't overtake
me, but I also know I don't have to do this on my own.*

A DESPERATE FATHER AND HIS SON

During quiet time not too long ago, God gave me new insight into
an old passage. In Mark 9:14-29, we learn about a desperate father
and his very troubled son.

Jesus and three of his disciples—Peter, James, and John—were
coming down a mountain after Jesus' transfiguration to meet with
the rest of the disciples. And there they were—flanked by a crowd
and midargument with some of the teachers of the law. When the
crowd saw Jesus, they rushed to him. Jesus was curious about the
argument and asked them what they were arguing about.

It was then that a voice rose from the crowd and explained that
his son had been possessed by a spirit. The spirit was so powerful that
it robbed him of his speech, seized him, and threw him to the ground
at times. He also complained that he had asked his disciples to drive
the spirit out of the boy but that the disciples could not. A little
tattletale-y if you ask me, but hey, Jesus did ask.

After responding to the father's criticism and calling his disciples
faithless (ouch!), Jesus turned his attention back to the father and
asked him to bring the boy to him. It was time to do the Jesus thing.
The passage tells us that as soon as the spirit in the boy saw Jesus, it
threw the boy to the ground and convulsed him.

To this, Jesus asked the father a simple question: "How long has he
been like this?"

The father answered plainly: "From childhood" (Mark 9:21).

And this, family, is where God gripped my spirit a little bit. This
seemingly insignificant part of the story. Because God's Word caused
me in that moment to reflect on the things I've dealt with "since

childhood." The memories that haven't yet faded. The names of people in my past who still send shivers down my spine. The chip on my shoulder that sometimes feels like a boulder. The parts of my being that I just assumed would always be there.

I believe God gave me this revelation for a reason. I wonder if you have hurt so deep for so long that you don't even recognize your pain as pain any more. It's just a part of you. As much a part of your day as your morning coffee or breakfast tea. Your pain might rise and fall as inconspicuously as you breathe. Unchecked, unexamined pain might have become central to your identity.

It's not that you've refused to take it to God or rejected him. Maybe it's more that you never realized this was an option. Maybe you haven't had a reason to believe your healing is a possibility. But I want to tell you that God doesn't just save souls. He heals them. Your open wounds can become healed scars. Your healed scars can reveal a triumphant story. It doesn't have to be how it's always been.

TYPES OF TRAUMATIC EXPERIENCES

Trauma is the Greek word for wound. Simply put, trauma refers to the painful physical, mental, and emotional wounds we are left with after experiencing a traumatic event. While there's an ongoing conversation around what exactly constitutes a traumatic event, there are some universal effects, including fear and anxiety; guilt and shame; grief; depression; anger; feelings of hopelessness, helplessness, and powerlessness; a changed worldview; a changed view of self; and difficulty trusting, communicating, or feeling safe in relationships. Moreover, trauma, at least initially, feels like an overwhelming inability to cope with life after trauma and with the event itself. Trauma can debilitate us.

The National Child Traumatic Stress Network has worked to articulate various types of traumas based on the nature of the event, who is involved, and what the law has to say. Table 3.1 is a summary of their findings. Keep in mind that this list is by no means exhaustive, but it can be a great start for being able to identify your own experiences and name your pain.

Table 3.1

Types of Traumatic Experiences
Physical Abuse or Assault: Actual or attempted infliction of physical pain with or without use of an object or weapon and including use of severe corporal punishment.
Sexual Abuse or Assault: Actual or attempted sexual contact, exposure to age-inappropriate sexual material or environments, sexual exploitation, unwanted or coercive sexual contact.
Emotional Abuse/Psychological Maltreatment: Acts of commission or omission, other than physical or sexual abuse, that have caused mental or emotional disturbance, such as verbal abuse, emotional abuse, excessive demands on a child's performance that may lead to negative self-image and disturbed behavior. Acts of omission against a minor child that caused or could have caused conduct, cognitive, affective or other mental disturbance, such as emotional neglect or intentional social deprivation.
Neglect: Failure by the child victim's caretaker(s) to provide needed, age-appropriate care although financially able to do so, including physical neglect, medical neglect, or educational neglect.
Exposure to Domestic Violence: Exposure to emotional abuse, actual/attempted physical or sexual assault, or aggressive control perpetrated between a parent/caretaker and another adult in the child victim's home environment or perpetrated by an adolescent against one or more adults in the child victim's home environment.
Victim of/Witness to Community Violence: Extreme violence in the community, including exposure to gang-related violence.
Victim of/Witness to School Violence: Violence that occurs in a school setting, including school shootings, bullying, and classmate suicide.
Victim of/Witness to Extreme Personal or Interpersonal Violence: Includes extreme violence by or between individuals, including exposure to suicide, homicide, and other similar extreme events.
Traumatic Grief/Separation: Death of a parent, primary caretaker or sibling; abrupt, unexpected, or premature death of a close family member, relative or close friend; abrupt, unexplained separation from a parent, primary caretaker, or sibling.
System-Induced Trauma: Traumatic removal from the home, traumatic foster placement, sibling separation, or multiple placements in a short amount of time.
Serious Accident or Illness, or Medical Procedure: Unintentional injury or accident, having a physical illness or experiencing medical procedures that are extremely painful and/or life threatening.
War, Terrorism, or Political Violence: Exposure to acts of war, terrorism, or political violence, including bombings, shootings, looting, or accidents that are a result of terrorist activity.
Forced Displacement: Forced relocation to a new home due to political reasons, generally including political asylees or immigrants fleeing political persecution.
Natural or Manmade Disasters: Major accident or disaster that is an unintentional result of a manmade or natural event.[1]

[1] "Trauma Types," The National Child Traumatic Stress Network, www.nctsn.org/what-is-child-trauma/trauma-types.

CHILDHOOD TRAUMA

All trauma is terrible, but the effects of trauma that we experience in childhood tend to be more pervasive and long-lasting. As children, we're still figuring out how the world works. We're working hard trying to make meaning out of our experiences. We are writing an internal script for how our future relationships will play out and developing a set of expectations, good and bad, for how people in our lives will treat us.

For some, this may mean withdrawing and avoiding people throughout the rest of your childhood and during adulthood because you've figured out that if you move alone in the world, then no one can touch you. For others, this may mean using power, control, and violence with others, because if you can make people feel small, they'll be too weak to hurt you. For others, this may mean being passive or unnecessarily submissive, because if you can deny your own needs and keep everyone else around you happy, then hopefully they'll be too satisfied to ever reject or abandon you.

Childhood trauma affects the brain as well. When children experience trauma, the brain releases stress hormones—namely, cortisol, adrenaline, and norepinephrine—which are a part of our fight-or-flight system and help our bodies respond effectively to threats. But when trauma persists—the parents won't stop fighting or the bullying endures—the brain overproduces these hormones, which can cause damage to the brain.

As one example of this, too many stress hormones in a child's brain can interfere with the development of structures in the brain important for cognitive skills—problem solving, decision making, language, social judgment, and emotional expression, to name a few. In adulthood, this may look like difficulty making decisions, judging social situations accurately, or expressing feelings in a relationship. This is not to say that these skills can't be learned or strengthened.

They can and should be. But if you share these difficulties, I encourage you to show yourself compassion. You've done the best you can with what you have.

BIG-T AND LITTLE-T TRAUMA

Some terrible experiences appear to be universally traumatic—for example, abuse, combat, or death. Some terrible experiences will vary in impact. Siblings, couples, family members, and friends may endure the same exact traumatic event but be affected in completely different ways. That's the nature of trauma. It's a highly personal, subjective experience that is influenced by our internal makeup and unique ways of processing information. For this reason, many mental health professionals have embraced the idea of big-T Traumas and little-t traumas as a way of validating the personal experiences of all their clients.

Big-T Traumas are a response to the events more commonly associated with the development of Post-Traumatic Stress Disorder (PTSD). These events involve actual or threatened death, serious injury, or a violation of bodily integrity. Sexual abuse or assault, physical abuse or assault, combat, serious accidents, and direct exposure to a natural disaster would all be considered big-T Traumas.

Little-t traumas aren't these, but are still highly distressing. They can exceed our ability to cope in the moment and disrupt our emotional functioning. Some examples of these would be emotional abuse, bullying or harassment, divorce, conflict, infidelity, loss of a significant relationship, and poverty or financial difficulty, to name a few. These traumatic incidents may not be inherently life threatening, but they do threaten and negatively affect our sense of self. Interestingly, the research in this area has indicated that repeated exposure to little-t traumas can cause even more emotional damage than exposure to a single big-T event.

IS THIS TRAUMA OR IS THIS HURT?

Both hurt and trauma cause emotional and mental pain. Thus, you may wonder if the pain and distress you're experiencing in the moment is the effect of trauma or hurt. This is an important question. The ability to identify, acknowledge, articulate, and understand how we feel empowers us. It enables us to begin to direct our healing to what we feel and need.

The next chapter is about hurt, so we'll spend time diving into that more there, but for the sake of clarifying and understanding our trauma, I want to provide brief distinctions between the two.

- Hurt affects us in the present. Trauma's impact is from the past.

- Hurt changes us temporarily. Trauma can change us permanently.

- Hurt hangs over our current worldview. Trauma hangs over our future.

- Hurt can naturally resolve with time. Trauma, however, doesn't typically resolve automatically and usually takes some intentional work.

- Hurt often points back to trauma. Trauma is the original wound.

In short, your pain could be trauma, your pain could be hurt, or your pain could reflect both. Ultimately what matters is that you understand how pain is operating in your life and seek to heal it.

HOW TRAUMA CHANGES US

Trauma doesn't just hurt us, it changes us.

Recall the stories of Audrey and British. Audrey spoke of crying out to God and feeling lonely and abandoned by him at a time she needed him the most. Her faith had been tried. British spoke vulnerably of experiencing anxiety, guilt, and depression after her brother's death, and becoming a person for a while who she didn't like.

Berto's story is another example of how trauma changes us. Berto was an eleven-year-old I worked with years ago at a trauma clinic for kids. Berto's dad had brought him in shortly after he and his wife, Berto's stepmother, separated. Berto's schoolwork was suffering, he wasn't sleeping, he wasn't eating, and he would say things like "Why should I get to eat when there are other children in the world who can't afford to?" This was an eleven-year-old kid, mind you. Who thinks about global poverty at age eleven?!

Berto also complained of bad stomachaches. Dad had taken Berto to see his doctor numerous times, but nothing seemed to be wrong. Dad had a gut feeling that this was psychological in nature. He was right. A month into therapy, the cause of pain was revealed: unbeknownst to Dad, Berto's stepmother had been physically abusing him.

Through vivid drawings and quiet words, Berto shared his memories of his stepmom beating him into submission whenever she wanted him to do something—wash the dishes, clean the kitchen, arrange her stuff, you name it. Berto would do his best to satisfy her, but a child's best is never good enough for an abusive parent. Berto would get locked in the closet and be told how bad of a kid he was. He was told he didn't deserve dinner. This led to Berto's struggle with trauma-related guilt. In his mind, *of course* he was a bad kid. Why else was he being beaten?

Fortunately, over time, Berto was able to see that his thoughts and feelings about himself had been hijacked by his trauma. He was a great kid who deserved love and protection. All kids did. He had no reason to feel guilty about anything despite what his stepmother's words and actions tried to make him believe. As these new beliefs began to sink in (which took months), Berto's issues gradually resolved, including the stomachaches. It appeared that Berto was physically manifesting the pain that was in his heart. Oh, the many ways trauma can infiltrate our lives.

- Trauma can affect our thought life and beliefs. It can change the patterns of our thinking and alter our view of ourselves and our world.

- Trauma can wreak havoc on our emotional life. It can fill us with sadness, grief, anger, rage, guilt, shame, fear, and disgust. It can make us feel worthless.

- Trauma can trigger serious mental health struggles such as depression, anxiety, PTSD, substance abuse problems, and more.

- Trauma can change personality.

- Trauma can affect relationships.

- Trauma can affect our view of God and our faith.

WHEN THOSE WHO ARE SUPPOSED TO LOVE YOU WOUND YOU

God gave certain people in our lives the responsibility of loving us, and the responsibility of taking care of us and protecting us from harm. These are the ones who are supposed to be the barrier between us and the cruel, dark world. These are the people who are supposed to fight our first battles with us. So what happens when they don't?

There is an even deeper pain you experience when the people in your lives who are supposed to protect you are the very same ones who expose you to harm. It was never meant to be that way. This was not in God's plan for you. But for many of you, this is the way it was.

Awhile back, God gave me a word for people like Audrey, Berto, and others who survived abuse from people they knew and trusted. It may be an encouragement to some of you. This word came from Ezekiel 34.

The word of the LORD came to me: "Son of man, prophesy against the shepherds of Israel; prophesy and say to them: 'This is what the Sovereign LORD says: Woe to you shepherds of Israel who only take care of yourselves! Should not shepherds take care of the flock? You eat the curds, clothe yourselves with the wool and slaughter the choice animals, but you do not take care of the flock. You have not strengthened the weak or healed the sick or bound up the injured. You have not brought back the strays or searched for the lost. You have ruled them harshly and brutally. . . .

"'Therefore, you shepherds, hear the word of the LORD: This is what the Sovereign LORD says: *I am against the shepherds and will hold them accountable for my flock.* I will remove them from tending the flock so that the shepherds can no longer feed themselves. I will rescue my flock from their mouths, and it will no longer be food for them.'" (Ezekiel 34:1-4, 9-10, italics added)

When I came across this passage and studied it, the words lifted off the page for me. I heard these words as a love letter. I read them like a promise letter. It was something that crushed spirits could hold on to. So I want to share these words with you. My prayer, though, is that you'll only hear what God wants you to hear.

As I sat with this passage, I heard God say:

I know you've been hurt. I know you're angry and confused. You've been through what most people couldn't bear. You've suffered great losses and you've mourned. You've grieved parts of yourself that your experiences took from you forever. You've tried to forgive, but you could never forget. I know. I see you. I feel your heart.

I know you've wondered where I was. I know you've wondered why it had to happen this way. I know you're searching for answers that you know deep down could probably never satisfy you. I chose fierce love for you and they failed you. I chose protection and security for you, but they were the ones you needed protection from. You didn't deserve it. You didn't deserve any of it.

But if there is one thing I need you to know now, one thing I plead that you never forget, it's this: I was against them. I am against them. I'm against what they did to you. I'm against how they treated you. I'm against the wounds that they left you and all the ways they made you hurt. When they touched you, they touched me. When they failed you, they failed me. When they betrayed your trust, they also betrayed mine, because I trusted them with you. I am against them and they will have to answer to me.

Don't wield this anger on your own. Share it with me. Don't stuff this pain deep down. Bring it to me. Don't seek revenge. It will only keep you attached to them. Trust me when I say I've got it. I will hold them accountable. I will bring justice in time. I will redeem. It's time for you to heal. Leave the rest of it to me.

I don't know who this is for. I may not ever. But I know that God loves you and has a message for you. Listen in. What do you hear him say?

WHAT'S YOUR STORY?

Let's get back to the story of the desperate father and his son. As I chewed on this passage, I had a "wait a minute" moment. Because this was Jesus. The Son of God. The reflection of God. God incarnate. The human form of our all-knowing, ever-present Father. Didn't he already know how long this boy had suffered?

Of course he did.

But that wasn't the point. Jesus wasn't seeking intel on the boy's medical history. He wasn't conducting a clinical interview like we mental health professionals have to do because we really don't know who is sitting in front of us in our therapy offices. No, Jesus was inviting this desperate, tired father to share his story. That's what Jesus does. He invites you to pour your heart out and give those memories back to him.

The enemy works in silence. He will work his hardest to make sure that you feel hopeless and alone. He will try his very best to keep you bound to your pain. He will make giving up attractive to you or cause you to believe that you—how you are right now, how you feel right now, what you see in yourself right now—will always be this way.

Healing requires that you tell your story. That is, at some point, and only somewhere you feel safe, it will be important for you to share your trauma. You need to open the story back up. You need to examine the wounds it gave you—in the form of messages, beliefs, ideologies, feelings—and reverse course. You need a new story. One that doesn't deny what happened to you, but one that has hope, strength, and a more accurate view of yourself, the world, and God.

If you have been exposed to big-T traumatic events, it is my recommendation that the time and place you tell your story is during a therapy session with a mental health professional. Open emotional wounds are beastly. Reopening wounds that you've worked for so long to tie up and heal on your own can be even more complicated. In the process of trying to finally take care of yourself, I want you to actually take care of yourself. This is what therapy is for.

But if you are ready to talk about your trauma (big-T or little-t) and have leaders or loved ones who you trust and who make you feel safe, sharing with them might be an okay place to start. Do pay attention to how you feel as you share. Notice if you're feeling more peace or becoming more restless. Notice if you're feeling freer or growing angrier or more agitated. Notice if you're feeling overwhelmed by your pain. These negative reactions may be signs that you need additional support.

Once you feel ready, know that there is no right way to tell your trauma story. There are only different parts to examine. Like Audrey and British, what's important for your healing is that you share what happened, how it affected you, and what you want for yourself moving forward.

Here are a few questions that can help guide you:

- *What happened?* What do you remember happening? Did this incident happen once, several times, or was it ongoing? What details stood out to you?

- *What were you thinking and feeling?* What feelings came up for you during the event? Fear? Guilt? Shame? What feelings crept up later or unexpectedly? What thoughts swarm in your head about the event now?

- *What was the impact of the event?* How long have you been hurting? How deep have you been hurting? Where do you feel this pain? Mentally? Emotionally? Spiritually? In your body?

- *What has changed?* What's changed about the way you look at yourself, others, or the world? What's changed about the way you view God? Has your pain affected your relationships?

- *What do you want now?* What would a healed you look like? What would freedom look like? What requests do you have for the people in your lives now? Do you have any requests of God?

FINDING PURPOSE IN PAIN

I'm going to admit something now you may disagree with. You may even slam this book shut. But I'm going to share it anyway: I don't believe that everything happens for a reason.

If this distresses you, I get it. I have been an active member of the church my whole life. I've listened to the church people say time and time again that there is a reason for everything and that God is behind it. I understand the appeals to trust God in his sovereignty and wisdom. I know that God is ultimately in control and wholeheartedly agree he has a lofty plan for our lives.

But I've also seen a whole lot. I've been in the trenches with victims of rape, sexual abuse, and harrowing family violence. I've cried alongside children who've lost parents and parents who've lost

children. I've interceded for friends when loved ones get their ter-
minal illness diagnosis. I literally know of kids raised like dogs.

That these things all happened for some "reason" never worked for
me. A reason has a why, and I never knew a person who could find
one for these things. A reason also has a reasoner, and if that person
was supposed to be God, well then God seemed quite cruel. The only
image these ideas conjured up for me was God sitting up on his
throne, premeditating pain for his children. Or God at his vision board
cutting up images of school shootings, helicopter crashes, and abuse.
If God wanted to somehow teach us a lesson or cause us to draw
nearer to him, I'm sure in his infinite intelligence and creativity, he
could have found a few other ways.

I much more resonate with the speculations that suffering is a con-
sequence of a fallen world and free will. For reasons we may appreciate or not, God has set this world up so humans are free to do what
they wish. And for reasons that may comfort us or not, this means
bad things may happen to us or our loved ones, and he may allow it.
God doesn't cause us pain, but the sin and brokenness of humankind
will. It's kind of all part of the human package.

But here's one really positive thing about that human package:
purpose.

See, I don't believe everything happens for a reason, but I do believe that in everything we can find purpose. God has given us the
ability to create purpose out of our pain. In fact, God himself does this
for us. I believe this message is what is at the heart of Joseph's words
when he said, "You intended to harm me, but God intended it for
good to accomplish what is now being done, the saving of many lives"
(Genesis 50:20). Or when Paul said in Romans 8:28, "And we know that
in all things God works for the good of those who love him, who have
been called according to his purpose."

I don't know who or what is behind your pain and trauma, nor do
I want to believe something easy. But I do know God says he will take

it all and cause good to happen to us regardless. He will create some good out of it. If we let him.

SHARING PURPOSE WITH FRIENDS

For five years, I co-led a nonprofit called the Ruby Project that I started with my sister and a few friends. Finding purpose was the focus of it. Everyone on the team had a story. Among us we had survived emotional abuse, sexual abuse, bullying, the death of siblings and parents, father abandonment, serious injury, and even sex trafficking, among other things. We were a group of survivors.

We were all also women of faith who worked in various health-related capacities and who found power in the creative and performing arts. Our commonalities made our mission clear: we would create a camp for girls where we would offer both medical and psychological support, give them the opportunity to express and retell their traumas through art, and share our faith with them, hopefully filling them with hope.

Let me tell you, that season gave the team and me some of the most transformative, transcendent, and meaningful moments of our lives. It changed the course of many of the girls' lives too. For a few reasons we had to take an extended hiatus, but by God's grace, we'll be back.

I don't know where you are in your healing journey, but if trauma is part of your story, take heart. With the freedom of God, we can find new meaning and even new beginnings. We can find joy and cause joy in others. We can aspire to inspire the hurting people around us, especially those who share our same scars. And that, my friends, is purpose.

THE QUESTION OF FORGIVENESS

Finally, forgiveness. Don't worry, I'm not going to tell you that you need to forgive. It's not what you need to hear right now. And you're probably already familiar with the Scriptures. You know that it's a religious and spiritual ideal.

But I do want to tell you what I've learned and taught about forgiveness. Perhaps it will clarify your path forward and empower you to make the best decision for yourself right now.

First, what forgiveness is not.

Forgiveness is not acceptance or reconciliation. It isn't saying "It's okay," nor is it saying "Hey, let's be friends again."

I'm not thrilled to admit it, but I've been on the unfortunate receiving end of this. I had to say goodbye to a friendship. Not because she hurt me, but because I hurt her. Three years before the end, she reached out and asked to share some concerns with me. When we met up, she was kind, she was tearful, but she was honest. Apparently the way I'd been handling certain things in our friendship had been a source of pain for her, triggering some old wounds of her past. I imagine she believed I could handle the conversation. I was a big sister figure to her, and we had been through a lot together. But unfortunately I was not able to handle this conversation in that season. I responded to her out of hurt and what I later realized were hints of toxic shame. In my defensiveness, I suggested to her that if this is the way I was making her feel, we should end our friendship. Then I shut her out of my life for almost two years.

Two years later, I visited a church I didn't realize she attended. As I turned the corner, there my friend was. My heart burst. Soon we were embracing each other with love. It felt so good. Later that week, I reached out. It seemed like it was time to make amends. I didn't hear from her for a couple of days, and when I did, I got this: *It was so good to see you and I've got so much love for you, but I am not at the place where I can sync up. I wish you the very best.*

I believed in my heart that she had forgiven me, but she was not interested in reconciling our friendship. I was disappointed but also strangely proud. She'd become a woman who could respectfully assert what she needed and wanted, and loving her meant loving that. I felt peace that God would continue to work on us both.

Forgiveness doesn't mean reconciliation. You don't have to be in a relationship that you're not ready or willing to be in again.

Forgiveness is a decision you make to let go of what's owed to you. In one of my favorite TED talks, speaker Sarah Montana shares her journey of how she came to forgive the young man who murdered her mother and brother.[1] To be honest, I don't know too many people, including myself, who could keep up with her there, but I love the way she describes forgiveness: "Forgiveness is only right when waiting for what we're owed comes at too high a cost."

When people hurt you, they create debt toward you. They put themselves in a position to owe you something—an explanation, an apology, the return of something they took from you, or the need to make amends. But what if what they owe you isn't tangible? What if what they took from you can't be replaced or returned? Like time. Or painful memories and emotional scars. What if that explanation you've been waiting on or the honest apology never comes? Therein lies the problem. Some debts are too great to repay.

This is the power of forgiveness. Forgiveness acknowledges that you're ready to move on without what's owed to you. It's saying: "This is what you did to me and this wasn't okay. But this will no longer hold me captive. I will heal myself with God. I need nothing else from you." This can happen in the form of a conversation, a letter, or just something you say and commit to yourself. Nobody even has to know.

Forgiveness unhooks you from the pain that people caused you. It weakens the grip of hurtful words, broken promises, and rejection tied around your neck. It celebrates a new chapter. If the person you're forgiving is someone you're choosing to keep in your life (in marriage, this will need to happen a hundred times over), your new season is a fresh start together. But if the person you're forgiving is gone or someone you're choosing not to reconcile with, your fresh start begins without them. Either way, forgiveness is freedom.

Forgiveness must happen at the right time. As powerful as this all is, forgiveness can't happen in the height of anger, rage, and resentment. That is just the psychological truth. Nor can it happen in the depths of our sadness. These feelings take up the emotional and psychological energy we need to be able to do the work. Forgiveness is a psycho-spiritual process that requires as much psychological preparation as it does spiritual conviction.

This doesn't make these heavy feelings terrible either. Emotional bitterness, for example, has purpose. As long as we feel it, we avoid the person who caused it. This appropriately keeps us at an emotional distance long enough to create a plan that will minimize further pain and distress. Of course, the great task here is to eventually do what we know God would want us to do, but that's a decision I'll leave to you and him. The point is, these types of feelings do have their place. They give us a little space to breathe and think and realize what we need to move forward.

Getting to the space where you're ready to forgive takes time. My hope is that within the love, compassion, and grace of God, you give yourself a little permission to take it. Then, when you're ready, I pray for strength to truly let your pain go.

4

HURT

Our Need to Recover What's Lost

Someone I loved once gave me a box full of darkness.
It took me years to understand that this too, was a gift.

MARY OLIVER

It is in dialogue with pain that many beautiful things acquire their value.

ALAIN DE BOTTON

We need never be ashamed of our tears.

CHARLES DICKENS

Don't allow your wounds to turn you into a person you are not.

PAULO COELHO

You keep track of all my sorrows.
You have collected all my tears in your bottle.
You have recorded each one in your book.

PSALM 56:8 NLT

MARY'S STORY
EVERY DAY, SOMEBODY CALLED ME UGLY

There was a point in my life that every day, somebody called me ugly. Granted, I was scrawny, and I didn't know how to style myself well or do my hair. But being made fun of for those things was nowhere near as painful as being made fun of for something I could never change. I was a Black girl with very dark skin, and there was nothing I could do about it. That was the most frustrating thing. Back then, there weren't any Love Your Skin campaigns or any dark-skinned celebrity women to really look up to. There was no Lupita. I learned to hate how I looked and had to face this all on my own.

They would say, "Who left you in the oven too long? Why is your skin so burnt? You look crispier than a burnt piece of chicken." They were relentless. Weirdly enough, some of them looked just like me; they were just lighter. Colorism is a real problem. I was a smart girl, so my teachers doted on me. But as a kid, what matters most to you is what your peers think. I was picked last for everything. I was teased in the cafeteria. I did have a few friends, but they didn't really know how to help me.

I grew up and left these people behind me. However, their words still stuck. I remember still struggling to take pictures for a while, or using apps when I did take them to brighten my skin. I tried skin lightening products at one point, but when they started breaking out my skin, I stopped. I couldn't be dark and rashy! I felt stuck with something I learned I shouldn't love.

SEYI'S STORY
I'D BEEN HURT BY GOD

I was in my last semester of grad school and extremely excited. I was months away from living my best life as a newly minted MBA grad. Then I got the call that would change the entire trajectory of my life: my mom had been diagnosed with stage 4 uterine cancer. Cancer. I never,

ever thought this word thrown around could affect someone so close to me, let alone my mother. But I kept my faith. I prayed, fasted, prayed some more. I read my Bible, got down on my knees, and worshiped like never before.

But that wasn't enough. Five months after her diagnosis, I saw my mom lying in her deathbed, body emaciated, face sunken, life . . . gone. I couldn't process what I was feeling at that moment. All I could do was to lay myself across her body and weep. How could this happen? My mom. The minister, sister, friend, giver, encourager, and prayer warrior. My everything. This was beyond unfair. I was inconsolable.

How dare God take my mother away from me? I was mad, angry, upset, and disappointed. I was hurt. I'd been hurt by God. If he could do this, then what was the point of believing? My pain manifested in many ways: I distanced myself from loved ones. I tried to consume myself with work. I cried myself to sleep, cried in my dreams, cried in my car, and cried while eating. My entire belief system had come crashing down, and I wanted nothing to do with my Creator.

THE HOLE IN OUR HEART

As imperfect people in an imperfect world, I think we all know hurt is an inevitable part of human experience. However, it doesn't mean we know how to deal with it very well. Instead, we do a number of things that not only don't heal us but also create more problems for us down the line.

We try to ignore it.

We try and deny it.

We try to distract ourselves from it with social media and entertainment.

We try to suppress it.

We try to numb it with food (especially sweets), alcohol, legal or illegal drugs.

We project it onto others.

We turn on the people who've been there for us and have made us feel safe.

We make other people accountable and responsible for fixing our pain.

Sometimes we do these things without realizing it. Other times we're fully aware of our poor coping mechanisms but are too hurt to care.

DEEP NEEDS CREATE DEEP HURT

Why are we like this? Well, first of all, hurt hurts. But not because we're weak or anything like that. Hurt hurts because we have legitimate, fundamental, internal needs. God in his strategy and intentionality designed us this way on purpose. We thrive when our deep, fundamental needs are met. We hurt when they're not. Striking this balance drives us to create and maintain relationships with each other. It also motivates our need to seek him.

Over the past sixty years, researchers have tried to enumerate what these deep needs are. Perhaps most notable are the works of psychologist Abraham Maslow, who suggested we have five deep needs (physiological needs, safety, love and belonging, esteem, and self-actualization), and of economist Manfred Max-Neef, who expanded on Maslow's work and proposed we have nine needs (subsistence, protection, affection, understanding, participation, recreation, creation, identity, and freedom).

Since Maslow and Max-Neef, clinicians, life coaches, and even ministers have distilled these classic theories in a way that reflects their own research, observations, and experiences working with their audiences. While they each put their own spin on it, there's great consistency with the needs that matter to us most. From my studies and observations, here's how I would summarize the list. We have deep needs for:

- *Safety and security.* We need to feel safe from harm, both physically and emotionally. This means feeling protected from bombs, hurricanes, and burglaries, as well as ridicule, shaming, and harassment.

- *Affection, connection, and belonging.* We need to feel like we belong somewhere and to someone. We need to feel wholly accepted for who we are. We need to feel the warmth of love and affection. We need to feel genuinely connected to people we care for, value, and respect.

- *Significance.* We need to feel like we matter in the world and to the people in our lives. We need to feel important. We need to feel needed. We don't want to feel like we're duplicates of somebody else. We need to feel distinctive.

- *Growth and realization.* We need to feel like we are growing and moving toward something. We need to see and feel progress. This explains our attraction to insight, awareness, and self-discovery. This motivates our pursuit of healing.

- *Contribution and creation.* We don't want to just take up space in the world while we're here. We are made in the image of God, and his first work was creation. We too need to create something that we can give in our lives, however symbolic. We need to feel like we are contributing meaningfully to our world.

Hurt is what happens when our deep needs go unfulfilled. It's the emotional fallout when these needs are disregarded, disrespected, or outright violated. Hurt, therefore, is self-protective. It acts as our first line of defense to psychologically threatening situations. Its goal is to alert us when there appears to be a problem in hopes of giving us a chance to fix things before permanent damage is done. Hurt feels like a hole in our heart . . . because it is.

HAIR TRIGGERS

Recall our discussions on the distinction between hurt and trauma in the previous chapter. Sometimes hurt hurts because it triggers old trauma. Sometimes it hurts because it reopens an original wound. The proof of this is often in our experience of current pain and in our reactions. For example, hair triggers.

If you've ever felt that you have overreacted to a situation, blown something out of proportion, or lashed out in anger at something small (which, let's be honest, we all have), then you know exactly what a hair trigger feels like. These are the types of reactions we have when some raw feeling is bubbling beneath the surface. Much of the time that raw feeling is our original wound.

In firearm terminology, a hair trigger is just a trigger that has an extremely short and light pull. This allows the slightest pressure on the gun to cause it to fire.

Emotional hair triggers work the same. When there is unresolved stuff in our lives, all it takes is one wrong look, one wrong word, or one wrong thing done to send us off in a tailspin. Within seconds, we're highly upset, distracted, distressed, and likely leaving everyone around us and even ourselves wondering what the heck just happened.

Though it may feel like it, and though you may even be accused of it, it's important to know you're not "crazy." However, your emotions (and your relationships) deserve a good, honest look. Hair triggers are an important way we become aware of the problematic core beliefs operating deep below the surface. They present an opportunity for us to look inside ourselves and see what still needs work.

Let's look now at the types of experiences that open up our hurt.

THE WAYS WE HURT

Words. "Sticks and stones may break my bones, but words can never hurt me." Fun fact: nobody believes this. Not you, not me, not psychotherapists, researchers, ministers, or mentors. Because not only have we all personally experienced the power of words in our lives—both good and bad—there's proof in the research.

In 2006, Martin Teicher, MD, and colleagues studied the relative impact of parental verbal abuse as compared to other abuses such as witnessing domestic violence, sexual abuse, and physical abuse while growing up on over five hundred young adults.[1] The results of the study showed that the effects of hurtful words by a parent had as a great an impact on these young adults as being exposed to these other abuses. Moreover, parental verbal abuse had an even greater effect than physical abuse alone.

In another one of his studies, Dr. Teicher and his team surveyed eight hundred young adults specifically about the impact of peer verbal abuse (verbal bullying) on mental health.[2] The study showed a link between peer verbal abuse and increased anxiety and depression, among other concerns. Interestingly, the effects of peer verbal abuse were compared to the effects of parental verbal abuse. Researchers found that when peer abuse occurred in middle school, it left the most severe mark. If you need some validation for the pervasive impact of childhood bullying on your life, there it is.

The implications are in Scripture too. We were created by words, as recorded in Genesis. "Let there be" was the beginning of our world, our earth, and our existence. God also literally gave us *his* Word. In his mind, the truth of his words in our lives would suffice. They would be enough to guide us, to comfort us, and to ward off the enemy much like Jesus did when he was tempted in the wilderness (Matthew 4:1-11). If that weren't enough to prove the power of words over our lives, the Bible spells it out explicitly. Proverbs 18:21 says: "The tongue has the power of life and death, and those who love it will eat its fruit." James 3:6 says, "The tongue also is a fire, a world of evil among the parts of the body. It corrupts the whole body, sets the whole course of one's life on fire, and is itself set on fire by hell."

There is certainly no mincing of words here. Words have power to heal us and destroy us. Words have power to lift us up and break us down. We can't blame ourselves for the impact of irresponsible and painful words on our lives. Words have the power to leave a mark.

Rejection. For a people who need and thrive off belonging and acceptance, we sure do face a lot of rejection in our lives. From being left out on the schoolyard to "we regret to inform you" letters. From being passed up for promotions to watching others get chosen over us. From having friends who "forget" to include us to being left for greener grass. Rejection hurts because we're not built for it. Belonging is all we've ever wanted. Though God has given us the strength to survive rejection, it will never be an easy thing to do.

Rejection's main casualties are our self-esteem and self-worth. These two concepts are often used interchangeably, but they are two different things. One of my favorite definitions of the two is provided by Dr. Christina Hibbert, who says: "Self-esteem is what we think and feel and believe about ourselves. Self-worth is recognizing 'I am greater than all of those things.' It is a deep knowing that I am of value, that I am loveable, necessary to this life, and of incomprehensible worth."[3]

The problem with rejection is that the experience feels contradictory to our own sense of value. Rejection creates thoughts like: *If I am really that great or really that lovable, then why doesn't he or she want me? If I'm really this valuable and have all this worth, then why won't these friends, this job, or this opportunity choose me?* In the heat of the moment, it's hard to see an alternative outside of *It must be me.*

But the truth is, there are so many reasons why rejection occurs. Sure, it can be on account of our own shortcomings at times—like in the case of job rejection—and this is okay. Sometimes we just need a bit more growth and development in some areas or skills. A no in our lives can simply be an opportunity to improve and try again. Our professional or personal lives are allowed to be assessed fairly to evaluate what we're bringing to the table or what more we could bring.

However, rejection is often not about us. Sometimes the reason we're rejected lies in the other person, like in the case of the bully who isn't happy or secure within themselves. Sometimes the reason is truly random, and it shouldn't be taken personally. And sometimes, yes sometimes, God allows rejection for our protection. For example, how many of us have been "rejected" by a lover only to be later down the line thanking God for removing us from that situation? Sometimes God allows a no in our lives so he can bring us to a better yes.

This isn't to say that rejection will ever be easy. Not at all. But I do know that once that initial sting fades—and it will—there will be an opportunity to reflect on the situation in a way that best honors yourself.

Disappointment. "How come he don't want me, man?" If like me you grew up on the nineties hit sitcom *The Fresh Prince of Bel-Air*, you may know exactly where this line comes from. In an iconic episode, Will's absentee father comes back into his life after fourteen years and works to win Will over. They plan a cross-country trip together, and Will gets really excited despite his uncle Phil's worried warnings. But who can blame him? He finally has a father again! We watch Will prepare for this trip and hope against all odds that his father shows up for him. Well, his father does show up, but only to tell Will that something's come up and he's got to leave for a while again. Another broken promise. The next moments are crushing as we watch Will try to use jokes to deny years of pain and disappointment until he can't anymore, crumbling into Uncle Phil's embrace. "How come he don't want me, man?" It's heart-wrenching, its impact far-reaching.

Every time this clip shows up in my timeline, I am reminded of just how many people resonate with the pain of disappointment. The pain we feel when our hopes and expectations for someone important in our lives go unfulfilled. Of course Will's story is an extreme example, one that has the pain of abandonment and rejection wrapped into it. But we've all dealt to some degree with people failing us or letting us down. And it's the worst when it's by the people we're supposed to believe in the most. These experiences leave memories that don't fade easily. These experiences leave shadows of doubt about the truth of our worth. They can also harden our hurt until it's unrecognizable.

Hardened hurt. I was working at a treatment facility for dual-diagnosis youth, and Arty was a sixteen-year-old client of mine. Dual diagnosis meant that the youth were coming in with two clinically significant concerns, namely, trauma and substance abuse. Arty had lived a long, hard life already, given his age, and he had been court ordered to our facility for his anger-management issues.

I wasn't totally prepared for the kid who walked in: a meth-using, car-stealing, pregnant-girlfriend-beating gang-banger who had tattooed devil horns at the top of his head. Then he opened his mouth: "Oh, you're Black? I told them I didn't want a Black therapist."

Lovely, I thought to myself.

I briefed my clinical supervisor right after my first session with Arty, which revealed much racial tension between his gang, a Hispanic gang, with Black gangs in the neighborhood. My supervisor recommended that I transfer Arty to someone else. He didn't want me to have to put up with this. But something about this kid tugged my spirit. I wasn't planning on becoming a martyr for this kind of client, but he felt like mine. I felt like God brought Arty to me for a reason. It was also clear to me that all of this crazed behavior was just a thick cover-up. Arty didn't have an anger problem. He had a hurt one.

After a few weeks of talking about everything in the world that made Arty mad (and a lot of things certainly did), he finally allowed us to talk about his home life. Arty watched his father beat his mother for years. While that in and of itself was distressing, what Arty hated his father even more for was later leaving them. Arty felt small for not being able to protect his mother, "which is what a man is supposed to do," he would say. But worse, Arty felt unloved. What kind of father abandons his kids?

Arty's mother now needed him to be the "man of the house." The strong one. But with no real role model for what that looked like, and no safe outlet for all that pain, it was all Arty could do to exert power and control in the cheapest of ways: rage, drugs, theft, racial prejudice, and gang violence. These discoveries became the focus of our work.

Sometimes anger is just the tip of the iceberg, under which more vulnerable emotions lie. This doesn't invalidate anger or relegate it as an emotion that doesn't have its own role or purpose. It just means that sometimes our anger is what we cling to in an attempt to hide or protect our confusion, sadness, and hurt. It's important to recognize when our anger isn't the real problem.

It took almost a year, but Arty eventually began to change. He stayed clean for six months, practiced empathy with his new kid, and had at least one Black woman in his life he respected. Right before his court date, he wrote me a letter saying, "Thank you for not giving up on me even though you had every right to." I was in tears.

Heartbreak. Heartbreak is also a form of rejection, but a dressed up form of it. In my opinion, it doesn't get talked about enough in the church and other contexts. Which one of us hasn't had to claw our way out of heartbreak?

They say that the average person experiences a broken heart at least twice in their lifetime. Anyone else thinking, *only twice?* I agree with recording artist Ashlee Simpson, who once said in an interview that you get your heart broken a million times in this life. However, you learn from each of those experiences. You grow from each of those experiences. You get over them and through them and find yourself much healthier and happier in the long run. While I'm not wishing an actual million heartbreaks on you, this is a good word. It doesn't make it any easier though. Especially when it is as biological as it is psychological.

In one study, Dr. Helen Fisher and a team of researchers out of Rutgers University found that romantic love could be broken down into three parts—lust, attraction, and attachment—which each produce distinct chemicals in our bodies.[4] Lust, the intense feeling of sexual desire, causes the release of testosterone and estrogen. Attraction leads to release of dopamine, a multipurpose chemical responsible for feelings of pleasure, and serotonin, a chemical heavily involved with sleep, appetite, and mood. This partly explains the exciting "I can't sleep, I can't eat" feelings we experience when we're falling in love. Finally, attachment—the strong feeling of connection we have with the people in our lives—leads to the release of vasopressin and oxytocin, two chemicals that help us create emotional bonds.

When heartbreak occurs, something else happens. These feel-good hormones drop, and cortisol explodes. Cortisol, as you may remember from a biology course, is our body's main stress hormone. It's the fuel behind our body's fight-or-flight response when we are threatened with danger. It's responsible for the surge of energy we feel when we barely escape a car accident or when we get a call that a loved one has been hurt. Cortisol levels rise to help us meet the demands of danger. Too much cortisol, however, derails us; it can lead to anxiety, unwanted weight gain, disrupted sleep, and a host of other health issues. Too much cortisol is the result of too much heartbreak.

A freshman tore into my office this past semester with puffy eyes and a flushed face. She'd missed my morning lecture, so I was happy to see her but also concerned by how she looked. "Dr. Amadi, I feel so ashamed." I was taken aback. What in the world had she done?

She then explained that her boyfriend broke up with her the night before. It was a toxic relationship, but the breakup still hurt. She had called her mom shortly afterward, who stayed on the phone with her all night. She got little sleep, slept through her alarm clock, and missed her morning practice and my 8 a.m. class. "I'm so sorry, this isn't like me," she kept saying.

I had to stop her, get her to catch her breath, and validate this incredibly normal reaction. Of course she wasn't herself. Her heart was breaking and her body was in chemical disarray. Which one of us can function well in that? It wasn't time to go into a chemistry lecture, but I comforted her and encouraged her to be gracious with herself. Heartbreak is utterly disorienting. She needed some time, space, and probably first some sleep.

THE BIOLOGY OF HURT

There's an even bigger picture here. Heartbreak isn't the only experience that creates havoc in our body. Rejection, rejecting words, disappointment, and abandonment do too.

Think about when you've been deeply wounded. You feel like you've been run over. Your body aches. You're bruised in places you cannot see or point to. You feel heavy, slowed, and lethargic. And even when that truck that ran you over is long gone, it's like something—and you don't know exactly what—is still weighing you down. You wonder why this hurts so bad.

Well, come to find out, your brain is actually in pain. The same parts of your brain that are activated when you are in physical pain—the anterior insula and the anterior cingulate cortex—are the same parts of your brain that are activated when you experience emotional or social pain.

Consider a study that looked at whether Tylenol, designed to relieve physical pain, could relieve social pain as well.[5] In this particular experiment, college students were randomly assigned to digest either 1000 milligrams of Tylenol a day for three weeks or digest a placebo. At the end of each day, the students completed a Hurt Feelings Scale to assess how their hurt was affected. Interestingly, those who took the Tylenol reported significantly less social pain over time as compared to the students who took the placebo. Tylenol literally made their hearts hurt less.

Important to note is that this study in no way, shape, or form intended to suggest that Tylenol be used to treat our emotional pain or social rejection. But it does support the idea that our brain registers social and emotional pain the same way it does physical pain. Hurt literally, figuratively, and biologically hurts.

HURT BY GOD

In Seyi's story, we heard the pain of a woman who felt like she had been hurt by God. Let's all be honest. Which one of us hasn't felt this way at some point in time? Like God himself had rejected us. Like God himself had forgotten us. Like he was the one we believed in and the one who ended up disappointing us. How many of us have felt that God is the reason for our pain?

I know I have. And I don't have a quick-fix response to those who've felt this way. All I can say is that feeling hurt by God is surely a universal experience. The stories are everywhere. What will matter in the end isn't that we've felt this way at times; it's how we choose to deal with it.

There's an incredible story behind the popular hymn "It Is Well with My Soul." Horatio Spafford was a prominent Chicago lawyer and businessman. He was also a devout Christian man who God had blessed with a wife and five children. Just as he hit the pinnacle of success, he and his wife lost their only son to scarlet fever. The following year, he lost all of his investments to the Chicago Fire of 1871. Despite overwhelming grief, his faith remained.

A few years later, Horatio decided to send his family on a much-needed vacation. They would set sail to England, and he would join them after wrapping up some business. Nothing could have prepared him for the telegram he received from his wife just a couple days after they left. "Saved alone" it read. The ship had collided with another vessel and gone under, claiming 226 passengers, including the rest of his four children. As a heartbroken Horatio left to meet his wife, he passed over the same sea that took everything from him. It was then that he penned the words that were later turned into a hymn:

> When peace like a river, attendeth my way,
> When sorrows like sea billows roll
> Whatever my lot, Thou has taught me to say
> It is well, it is well, with my soul.

I'm speechless every time I remember it.

It reminds me of a sobering conversation I had once with my own dad. I'll never forget it. I was going through a rough time and reached out to him, asking genuinely how he had been able to keep his faith for so long. He was a man in his seventies who had fought in wars, faced deaths, endured losses, seen prayers go unanswered, and had seemed at times to be holding the weight of the world on his shoulders. How did he do this? He simply said, "You need the kind of faith that won't fail you. You choose your type of faith."

It's something I still think about. Almost hauntingly. What is my faith based on? Does it allow for hardship, crises, losses, and uncertainty? Does it allow for hurt, rejection, and disappointment? Or will I jump ship when these things happen? What does it really mean to say that "God never fails"?

I can't say that my faith is at the place of Horatio's, or ever will be, but I can say with certainty that life has forced me to expand my understanding of faith. This is a deeply personal journey that we all have to take. My prayer is that wherever your journey leads you, you feel God is near.

GOD, WHERE ARE YOU?

We know the God of the Bible. The God who's cured the sick, healed the blind, stood between women and societal scorn, and raised people from the dead. The God who appears right when his children ask him to.

It's only natural that we expect to experience God the same way. That when we ask him to, he takes the pain away immediately. What's a measly heartbreak when you've raised people from the dead? So we cry out to him: *God, where are you? What can you do for me here?*

Most of the time, we don't get a big, booming answer. We don't see flaming arrows or fiery bushes. It doesn't seem like we've gotten anything at all. We call out again: *God, where are you?* Still no answer. Our posture begins to shift. We're frustrated by what feels like a non-response. We may call out yet again, but this time we're upset, skeptical, maybe even menacing. Our disbelief rises, and we consider taking things into our hands. We fantasize about our own vindication. We entertain revenge. We move away from our knowledge of God and his Word. We feel like God has abandoned us, so we start to abandon him. Maybe you've been here before.

But what I've learned about God in my own life is that in these moments he often moves more quietly. His actions are subtle and strategic. He gives us the space and the grace to freak out. He steadies us until we calm down. He waits until we're ready to receive from him. Then, when we are, his words become clear. It wasn't ever the case that he wasn't there. Psalm 34:18 says: "The Lord is close to the brokenhearted."

Take a moment and feel what that means to you. We too often run over some of God's best words and greatest promises. But when things go wrong, it's the simple things we first need. When we are sitting in the puddle of our own tears, God is close. When we can't make sense out of what just happened, God is close. When we wonder if the people who hurt us will ever truly know the weight of their words or actions, God is close. When we're not quite sure how to move forward, God is close. You may not feel him, but try and see him there. Picture him there next to you, because he is.

Remember the times in the past when you had no idea how you would pull through. God was close. Or how you got through a day of work though your heart shattered the night before. God was close. Think about how you were able to take care of family, friends, students, employees, and other people who depended on you though you had no strength. God was close. That was him walking alongside you. That was him holding you up. The God who held you together before will continue to do so.

This matters. We can't do much without the strength of God. God's closeness brings that strength. God's closeness brings us wisdom. God's closeness brings us clarity. God's closeness brings us comfort. God's closeness brings us peace. God's closeness is the beginning of our healing.

THE ART OF RECOVERY

To recover means to "return to a normal state of health, mind, or strength" or to "find or regain possession of something stolen or lost," according to the *Oxford English Dictionary*. I love how crystal clear these definitions make our goals for recovering from hurt. We certainly do need to find our way to health again—to a healthy mind, body, and spirit. We certainly do need to find our way to strength again. We certainly do need to recover the things that were lost and fulfill anew the deep needs we rightfully have. We can do this. We can do this with a few healing tools we can apply.

Self-soothing. Self-soothing is a psychological practice that helps us to calm our hearts and minds and pour back into ourselves. It's a form of self-love and self-compassion, and it's exactly what you need. The following steps will help you practice it.

1. *First, just feel.* Don't hold in or suppress your feelings. Find yourself a space where you won't need to. Find a place where you can just let yourself cry. Or sit and stare at the wall. Or exhale long and deeply. Notice where your feelings are— maybe in your stomach or your chest. Allow them to be there. Running over them or numbing them will only delay or complicate the process. Sometimes you will relive these moments for days, or on and off for weeks. But your feelings will naturally resolve. Deeper hurts may feel raw for months. In this case, your brain may need extra time to process. Give it that. We call this leaning in.

2. *Acknowledge your thoughts and feelings nonjudgmentally.* As you lean into your feelings, begin to acknowledge them: *I feel hurt. I feel angry. I feel betrayed.* Allow your brain to begin processing: *Man, I didn't get the job. Wow, we really just broke up. I can't believe they disappointed me again.*

3. Become mindful of what's going on in your head. *It seems like I fail a lot. It seems like I push everyone away. How could I have let*

him do that again? If I didn't _____, this wouldn't have happened. Because you're hurt, your thoughts are likely to take a dark, self-critical, self-blaming turn. Do your best to avoid this or to recover quickly, but if you find yourself still spiraling in that direction, just take notice of it. Don't further condemn yourself for it. Make a mental note that your thought life still needs a little work and just let it pass: *Okay, these are really negative thoughts, but this is what I'm feeling right now. I don't feel like this always. It's easy to feel like this right now. I will let this pass.*

4. *Employ a calming word or phrase.* When I'm in this space, I've found that gently telling myself, *It's okay, I'm okay,* and *It's all going to be okay* calms me. I've shared this with my audiences and those in my care and have heard that some use these exact words, and others find their own. I love hearing both. What's of utmost importance is to adopt and employ words that work for you. Once you do, I suggest you write them down in the front of your journal, or display them somehow in your room as a quick reference for when you really need them. Do this until it becomes second nature. I've also found that though I believe in turning to Scripture for comfort, I'm not inspired to do so until I've first calmed down. It's hard to be open and to receive, however good a word, in the middle of emotional implosion. Keep that in mind.

5. *Reach out to your soothing sponsor.* It's called "self-soothing," but sometimes you need a little help. You probably already have a soothing sponsor in your life. This is someone who you know won't judge you for your thoughts and intense feelings. This is also a person who can reflect your real self back to you. A person who can encourage, affirm, and help clarify things for you. This may also be a person who can pray with you if you wish. For me, it's my therapist (naturally), whom I can talk to

about most anything but probably wouldn't pray with. It's my mother and sister and family, whom I often do pray with. And it's a small number of friends I can turn to when I need to be reminded of who I am.

Emotional unpacking. Once you've soothed yourself, it's time to emotionally unpack. This is what it sounds like. Think of your healing journey, particularly after a hurtful incident, as though you're coming home between two big trips. You get home from one and know you've got to soon get ready for the other. So you shower, rest up a bit, then throw your suitcase on the bed and get to work. What did you wear? What needs to be washed? What got ruined on your trip and needs to be thrown out altogether? Most importantly, what are you putting back into your suitcase?

Emotional unpacking works just like this. It means separating healthy thoughts and feelings from the unhealthy ones. It means noticing what pain is today's and what pain is old. It means examining the impact of the hurtful words and actions on your mind and behaviors. It means measuring your next steps so you can heal.

When you're ready to unpack, ask yourself, *What thoughts do I want to keep? What thoughts need to be shaken? What thoughts do I want to throw away?* Then, take the thoughts that are honest and accurate and that truly serve you, and put only those in your suitcase.

Be fairer with yourself. We are meaning-making creatures. We are hardwired for it. We judge our different experiences and make a ruling about what we think they mean. Interestingly, we do this even when things have no inherent meaning or when things can take on several meanings. This process is automatic and happens instantaneously.

The problem is, when people hurt us, we filter our experiences through our problematic beliefs about ourselves. That means if we're already walking around with a deep-seated belief that we are difficult to love, for example, we will see people's actions through this lens. We won't think about or consider the dysfunction in the other person, or all the other factors that could have affected the final result. We will confirm our beliefs by saying, *See! This is why everybody leaves me! I'm too hard to love!*

We need to create better meanings out of our experiences. We need to be fairer with ourselves. This is hard work, especially since we operate, mostly unconsciously, with filters that we've built up since childhood. But we can make up our minds to become more aware. We can back away from the first meaning we give our painful experiences and become more intentional with our thinking. Healthy adults learn to take responsibility for their actions. But healthy adults also learn to be fair and loving toward themselves.

Go where you belong. This may go without saying, but in this sensitive time, you need to surround yourself with people who wholly and completely accept you. People who love your presence. People who are happy to claim you in their lives. People who make you feel like you belong. This helps us get our groove back and gives us the validation and affirmation we need to feel like we're somebody again. No hurtful words, rejection, disappointment, or heartbreak will define us. We may have lost our mojo for a bit, but we're not going to be without it for too long. Find the people who speak life back into you, and get your strength back. Recover from this and keep going. You've got a life to live.

LET GOD PUT YOU BACK TOGETHER

In Psalm 147:3 we read: "He heals the brokenhearted and binds up their wounds." The word "heal" in this psalm is the Hebrew word *rapha,* meaning "to heal, to sew together or mend" or "to make healthy." The words "bind up" are the Hebrew word *khabash,* which means "to tie, restrain, to bandage." This is incredible to me. It's a complete picture of healing. In my own Nigerian culture, you'll often hear church congregations sing and refer to God as "Doctor Jesus." I always felt they were onto something, and it appears they are.

Now some may take this literally and believe they don't have to do anything more than pray to be healed. This can work. But God in his infinite wisdom, foresight, and creativity has also given us the ability to heal each other and ourselves through restorative experiences, relationships, and community.

This is what healing looked like for Mary, who once learned to hate her skin:

I've healed over the years, and I have a lot of people to thank. Family who always told me I was beautiful. Friends who have celebrated every part of me. Dating experiences with men who've reveled in my melanin. Gatekeepers in the media who have pushed for new standards of beauty. We need even more of this. Feeling beautiful is a relatively new thing for me, but it matters. I no longer feel like I have to hide. I no longer feel like I need to be something or someone else to be worthy.

I'm thankful for these experiences and thankful to God. He's allowed me opportunities to see myself the way I know now that he sees me.

For Seyi, who lost her mom to cancer, her healing journey began as she sought a more direct encounter with God:

It's been a few years, and I am still hurt. I'm still confused. I still don't have any answers about why it had to be this way. But I'm learning how to live through this. I told God, "It's just me and you now." I told him that all I can do is to be honest about exactly how I'm feeling. No more beating around the bush, no more faking the funk, no more pretending to be okay when I'm not.

I know what my mom wanted for me: joy, happiness, peace, a life filled with God. But this hurt is my new base. I've had to start over. I've had to rebuild my relationship with God from scratch. I was willing. Perhaps that's the grace of God. My loss still hurts, but now it also guides me. I guess I wear it as a badge of honor of sorts. It reminds me I'm pushing through in spite of. Some days, the sun does shine.

As believers, we can expect that God will find ways to be present with us in our pain. We can also expect that he will work to make us healthy and whole again as he treats and bandages our wounds. Sometimes he'll touch our hearts directly. Other times, he'll work through a friend or community. No matter the method, healing is God's promise to us. It may take time, tools, love, and restorative experiences, but it's a promise.

DISCOURAGEMENT

Our Need for Confidence and Courage

*In spite of everything I shall rise again: I will take
up my pencil, which I have forsaken in my great
discouragement, and I will go on with my drawing.*

VINCENT VAN GOGH

*Every great work, every big accomplishment, has been
brought into manifestation through holding to the vision,
and often just before the big achievement comes
apparent failure and discouragement.*

FLORENCE SCOVEL SHINN

*We are pressed on every side by troubles, but not
crushed and broken. We are perplexed because we don't know
why things happen as they do, but we don't give up and quit.
We are hunted down, but God never abandons us. We get
knocked down, but we get up again and keep going.*

2 CORINTHIANS 4:8-9 LB

NATALIE'S STORY
FOR YEARS, I COULDN'T FIND A JOB

I was a fresh doctoral-level graduate with the brightest political future ahead of me. During my grad school years, I did everything "right." I had campaigned for Obama, worked on Capitol Hill, assisted a mayor, and volunteered at various political events across the country. I was sure that finding employment wouldn't be a problem and gave myself permission to dream big. With all the confidence in the world, I set my heart on a particular prestigious position and went for it. This would launch me into the political stratosphere. I was rejected. Though it stung, I couldn't say I was surprised. They were probably looking for someone with a little more work experience. So I cut my losses and focused on casting my net a little wider.

Three months later, nothing. I dusted myself off and cast even wider. Six months later and still nothing. I was discouraged, but things only grew worse. A year later I was still unemployed and running out of money. I decided to move nearer to my family because I needed their support. Support I did get, but I was not prepared for what the next few seasons of my life would present to me: absolutely nothing. An absolutely brutal, disillusioning, hope-failing nothing.

Two years passed by and I still couldn't find full-time, field-related employment. Three years passed by and still nothing. Sure, I'd found odd jobs and gigs that helped me put gas in my car, but I was a "doctor" in my field and couldn't get myself a career. Never mind the hundreds of applications I was sending out every year. When four, five, and six years passed by, my mind, body, and spirit had finally had it. I fell into a deep depression. Reflecting on that season now, I know that without God, my mother, my family's prayers, and some therapy, I for sure wouldn't be here.

THE LOSS OF HOPE AND CONFIDENCE

Like Natalie, you may know what it feels like to reach out desperately for something and come up short. You may know what it feels like to try and try again at something and still fail. You may even know the pain of an unanswered prayer. This is what it means to be human. This is what it means to live a life of faith.

Pastor Steven Furtick of Elevation Church got it right when he said during one of his services that "God's presence doesn't prevent us from trouble. It enables us to get through." I was relieved to hear him say this because too often, at least on some subconscious level, we expect that we will have *less* trouble because we believe in God. But if you sit down with the average Christian, or even if you reflect on your own life history, you know that's simply not true.

We are spiritually enabled in trouble—we are empowered, redeemed, restored, and all of our troubles are reworked for our purpose, blessing, and good. But we are not exempt from troubles. If anything, we become even more attractive to trouble because our faith and hope in Jesus is the most powerful thing on this earth. So, we face the trouble. We face the failures. We face what feels like empty promises from God. We face the pain of wanting, of needing, of feeling deserving but still being denied. We face the pain of discouragement.

To be discouraged is to be deprived of hope, confidence, and courage. It is to be disheartened or dispirited. The *Oxford English Dictionary* uses the same words to define discouragement but adds another worthy piece to its definition: *enthusiasm*. To be discouraged, it says, is to lose not only confidence and hope but enthusiasm as well.

Our goals and aspirations, our desires and dreams, our unique calling and purpose, and our basic needs all help define our existence. They create joy and meaning. But they also swing open wide the door to the pain of discouragement, since the road to fulfillment is hardly ever straightforward or easy. The delays challenge our hope. The setbacks threaten our confidence. The doubts creep into our hearts at night and convince us that we're not able. We're not capable. We're too old. Too young. Too different. Too awkward. Too far behind, not far enough, or altogether not worthy enough. Real love? That doesn't exist. Happy endings? That's for fairy tales. And even if the good things do exist, they must not for me. I've lost my chance. I've missed my shot.

THE LOSS OF COURAGE

Delays and setbacks rob our hope, confidence, and enthusiasm, and also rob our courage. The loss of courage is at the heart of discouragement. This is not something to take lightly. Without courage, we can't do hard things. Without courage we can't do anything at all. That's because courage is not just a decision; it's an *ability*.

Courage is the ability to persevere.

Courage is the ability to venture into new territories.

Courage is the ability to face our fears.

Courage is the ability to withstand adversity.

Courage is climbing to the top of Mount Everest, the highest mountain in the world. But courage is also working twenty-nine thousand feet below it, on the ground, serving alongside the Nepalese to spread the good news of Jesus.

Courage is when you go out on your first date in four years because your heart has finally healed after your failed marriage. But courage is also going out on your 222nd date as a never-married single woman, even though the first 221 dates didn't lead anywhere.

Courage is when you pray that God will heal a friend's mother from cancer when you just lost your own mom to it a year ago. Courage is praying and trying for a baby, even after you've been told it's just not possible.

Courage wakes us up and keeps us going. We can't live out our purpose, calling, and dreams without it.

HANNAH'S HOPE

I love being able to turn to the Word of God for inspiration, affirmation, and validation of our human experiences. When working with both students and clients, I love being able to merge research and academia with faith and Scripture and find where they meet. And when it comes to navigating discouragement, I love reflecting on 1 Samuel 1, where we find the story of Hannah.

In the story, we immediately learn that Hannah was married to a man named Elkanah. Elkanah loved Hannah deeply, but he was also married to a woman named Peninnah. What gives? Well, Hannah was barren. Theologians believe that though Hannah was Elkanah's one true love, he sought out and married Peninnah, who would be able to produce offspring for him. This obviously wouldn't fly today, but so it was in those days.

Peninnah was indeed a successful child-bearer. Verse 2 says, "Peninnah had children, but Hannah had none." Despite how many times I've read over this passage, I always pause at this verse. Because I can resonate with the tough reality of having a deep desire that seems to be in everyone else's hands but my own. Can't we all? I think of those who are praying for a spouse when all their friends are not only married but on their second, third, or fourth kid. I think of those staying up night after night, trying but struggling to bring success to their business. I think of those working their tail off to make rent while watching people half their age buy their first home. Hannah would understand. All she wanted was a child, but instead of getting her personal prayer answered, she got to watch Peninnah get hers.

But what made Hannah's story a true case of discouragement was the fact that this went on "year after year." Year after year, Hannah tried to get pregnant and couldn't. Year after year, Peninnah provoked her to tears about it. Year after year, Hannah's husband would try and console her, asking her, "Aren't I enough for you?" To which I imagine Hannah responding: "You are wonderful and I love you. But I just want my son." Year after year, the pain and frustration of an unmet desire remained.

During one particular trip up to Shiloh where she and Elkanah went to worship and sacrifice, Hannah let all her feelings out. Verse 10 tells us that in her "deep anguish," Hannah prayed to the Lord, "weeping bitterly." She made a vow to God that she would devote her son's whole life to the Lord if he would just give her one. Then she returned to prayer, silently, lips moving in such a way that when the presiding priest—a man named Eli—saw her from the doorpost, he called her out for being drunk! But Hannah cleared that up quickly and told him that she wasn't drunk, she was just "deeply troubled" and praying out of "anguish and grief." Hannah was disheartened. Hannah was dispirited. And though Hannah never stopped praying, Hannah was discouraged.

DOORWAYS TO DISCOURAGEMENT

My siblings and I grew up with two very amazing but very different parents. Mom was the nurturer, affirmer, and encourager, the person you wanted to go to if you were in distress or pain and needed your heart held. Dad was the one you went to after you got yourself together a little bit and needed a plan. If you went to Dad with tears still pouring out of your eyes, he would sit with you awhile quietly, and you would wait to see what he had to say, and the first words out of his mouth would literally be, "So what's the plan?" I know my siblings will laugh when they read this because that was him every time. Every single time.

His question would lead to some mutual brainstorming for how we could get out of the pain of our predicament. Then he would close the conversation by saying something to the tune of: "Remember, you weren't born with it, so you won't die with it. It will go away." While this obviously isn't true in every case, there is truth to it in many situations. What he was trying to say is that pain comes and goes. Pain is temporary. Don't get accustomed to your pain.

These words can also be applied to the experience of discouragement. We are not born with a predisposition for discouragement.

There is no genetic component to this experience like there often is with things like clinical depression or anxiety. Discouragement is situational. It arises from the experiences in our lives that leave us feeling dissatisfied, disheartened, and distressed. It can also arise from social and cultural crises such as racism, sexism, and injustice—these issues can often feel beyond our control.

Here's a short list of common "doorways" to discouragement:

- feeling overlooked or unnoticed
- feeling liked you missed your chance or shot
- feeling unappreciated
- being misunderstood
- unfair criticism
- rejection
- ridicule
- self-doubt and fear
- hurt and disappointment
- personal failure
- social, cultural, and political crises

Which of these resonate with you?

For Hannah, I imagine her hurt and disappointment every time she got to the time of the month when her body would tell her nope, not pregnant. I imagine that years of being provoked by Peninnah developed in her a thick skin and a solid poker face, but that behind closed doors and in a closet somewhere where her husband wouldn't see her, she would crumble to the floor in hurt and tears. I imagine that though her worship was real and her prayers persisted, there were moments when she was sure God had forgotten her. I imagine that as a woman in this particular time in history, Hannah felt like a failure.

THE FAILURE TO PRODUCE

There is something particularly painful about an inability to produce. There's the "soul-crushing, emotionally-crippling, relationship-destroying" pain, as writer Kylie Blenkhorn puts it, of being legitimately unable to bring a child into this world.[1] This kind of pain is in a class of its own and affects 10 percent of US couples according to recent stats.[2]

But then there's the felt failure to bring forth a vision or a dream, the failure to achieve a specific accomplishment, the failure to manifest the deep desires of your heart. These failures may be more common to us. I would even go as far as saying that one hundred out of every one hundred individuals have dealt with the painful effects of this.

Studies in the field of neuroscience have shown that the brain physically changes during failure. Literally. This physiology of failure is best understood by first understanding the physiology of success.

When we succeed, when we win at something, our brains increase the release of testosterone and dopamine—a hormone and a neurotransmitter. With time and repetition, the increase of these brain chemicals changes the chemistry of the brain, thereby making the winner more focused, confident, clearer, smarter, and more willing to take on risks. In short, the brain of a winner gets primed to, well, keep on winning. This has been referred to as the "winner effect,"[3] a term championed by Ian Robertson, researcher and author of the book by the same name.

The author puts it this way:

> The winner effect is something that happens across species of humans and animals. If you win a contest—it doesn't matter what kind of contest, it could be a chess match against someone who is not very good—the mere act of winning will make it more likely that you will win in a big, difficult context the next time. That's the most remarkable finding in human neuroscience.[4]

Losing is equally powerful. Studies show that when we experience a failure, our brains release cortisol—the same chemical our brains release under high stress. This in turn makes the person who has lost or failed more risk averse and more likely to avoid competition. How do you succeed when you avoid risk? Easy answer: you don't. All success requires an element of risk. All success requires courage. Whereas winning naturally leads to more winning, based on physiology alone, losing can naturally lead to more losing. That is, unless we do something about it.

FAILURE WOES

Failure also affects us psychologically. Repeated failure doesn't just threaten to take away our hope, confidence, and courage; it adds a unique set of troubles to our lives that digs us deeper into our experience of discouragement. These are what I call failure woes. Here are short descriptions of each of them.

Failure woe #1: fatigue. Failure fatigues us. You know what this feels like when you've worked and worked and worked, and you've strategized, and you've prayed and prayed some more, and you still come up short. Fatigue is the result of exhausting all of your energy for something you believe in and still not getting the results you deserve.

Failure woe #2: frustration. Failure frustrates us. Frustration is the feeling of being upset or annoyed because of a perceived inability to change or achieve something. The more important the goal, the greater the frustration. The more intimate the goal, the more deeply frustrating the failure is. Imagine Hannah's frustration. Frustration is a normal, healthy response to failure, but it can quickly turn into anger or great stress, or downward spiral fully into depression.

Failure woe #3: a sense of finality. Failure can also create in us a sense of finality. A sense that the reality we are experiencing now is the reality that will always be. Finality feels like you've come to the end. Go ahead and pull the plug on those prayers! God's over them. The unfortunate reality of reaching this point is that oftentimes, things come to an end for no other reason than because we've let them. Things conclude because we've made a conclusion. The curtain is pulled on a mere intermission. We've pulled the curtain and we've left it there.

Now, I do believe that after repeated failure, it's wise to rethink our approach. A new result typically requires a new action. But when we give in to the sense of finality, we rob ourselves of creating new pathways to our goals. We also rob ourselves of simple solutions like the need to rest. Maybe we just need a break. Maybe we just need some time and rejuvenation that will give us the renewed clarity, focus, strategy, and energy we need to go for the goal and get it this time.

Failure woe #4: forfeit. When you're fatigued, frustrated, and believing that your journey has come to an end, what choice do you have but to forfeit? That's the respectable thing to do. Unless, of course, God hasn't said it's over and it was all just a matter of time.

LEARN LESSONS, LOSE COUNT

There is a thin line between learning from your failures and fixating on them, and this makes all the difference in the world.

I hung out with one of my show-biz friends and mentors, Sheryl. Sheryl is a producer, show creator, and showrunner at Netflix. We sat down for lunch, caught up on our personal lives, and shared all the exciting developments in our writing careers (and by "our" I mean hers because she has a new show coming to Netflix and I, at the moment of writing this book, have a new show . . . to add to my Netflix list).

Naturally, I opened up to her about my discouragement around industry rejections. I'll never forget what she said to me: "Peace, you have to lose count of the noes. You just have to lose count. Act like they never happened." It's like she knew I needed to hear that because I'm not naturally a "lose count" type of person. I don't lose count of anything. In fact, not only do I not lose count, I recount. I ruminate. I remember every little thing of every last day and remember every single word that's ever been said to me. It's just how my brain works. But Sheryl was right. Lessons should be learned, but noes should be forgotten. No matter how many of them there seem to be.

Learning from your failures means extracting lessons from them. You didn't eat enough protein today and fainted during your workout? You better get your protein in tomorrow. You failed a college course because you never showed up to class? Show up next semester. You wrote a script, and it got rejected with a note that your protagonist got lost in the story? Rewrite the pages and make her shine. You got dumped because you didn't know how to appropriately communicate your emotions? When love comes around again, do the work necessary to be better. Talk to a relationship role model, get counsel from your mentor, read books on how to express yourself well.

Now to be fair, some of these things are easier said than done. The bigger the failure, or the greater the failure's impact (like, say, when your mistakes affect your family members or someone else you care about), the harder it can be to make a comeback. But just because it is easier said than done doesn't mean it's impossible. While it's okay to grieve such losses for a time (and you're allowed to be the judge on how long this grieving time should be), it doesn't serve you to beat yourself up. Take as long as you need to glean the lesson. Then move on.

KEEP ON KEEPIN' ON

There are questions about where the phrase "keep on keepin' on" originally came from, but it is pretty clear that it was popularized by Curtis Lee Mayfield when he wrote and performed a song of the same name. Mayfield was an African American award-winning singer-songwriter who rose to prominence during the civil rights era for his politically conscious soul music. His musical group—The Impressions—produced songs that became the music of a revolution.

Black students sang their songs as they protested outside their universities, freedom marchers sang their songs as they marched to jail, and Dr. Martin Luther King Jr. himself was so inspired that he adopted one of their songs, "Keep On Pushing," as the unofficial anthem of the civil rights movement. Mayfield became a musical hero for inspiring hope, confidence, and courage in the heart of Black America.

On August 13, 1990, Mayfield became paralyzed from the neck down after stage lighting equipment fell on him during one of his outdoor concerts in Brooklyn, New York. A freak tragedy if I've ever heard of one. But did this end his career? No. Though Mayfield was unable to play the guitar, he continued to record. Lying on his back, he recorded his vocals, line by line, until he completed his next album. He would go on to live another nine years past the accident, winning both a Grammy Legend Award and a Grammy Lifetime Achievement Award in the time. He would keep on keepin' on.

Allow me to give this to you straight. The antidote for your discouragement is to keep on keeping on. The key to overcoming is to keep on going. The courage to keep praying like Hannah, to keep trusting, and to keep working is what you owe to yourself. You must salvage the courage to see things through.

BUT FIRST, REST

The idea of rest may feel contradictory to the message of keeping on, but it's really quite crucial. If on the road to manifesting the dreams of your life, you grow tired, weary, or fatigued, know that it's okay for you to rest. In fact, I insist that you do because you cannot produce in a fatigued state. It doesn't matter whether we're talking about brainstorming a new business strategy, executing a new plan for dating, or preparing to have a difficult but crucial conversation to save your marriage. You cannot produce in a fatigued state.

Every fall in my Intro to Psychology course, I teach on sleep. This always ends up being one of my students' favorite lectures (maybe because they are no longer getting it?) and one that changes their lives for the better. That's because during this lecture they learn that staying up all night studying for an exam is actually working against them! To put it simply, sleep is when memory consolidation takes place. Though we take in new information during wakefulness, the process of actually committing that new information to memory happens while we are asleep. So going over that study guide through the night and up until the exam? Far less effective than studying up until the point when you can get a good night's rest.

Even more significant is the fact that when we lose much-needed sleep, our neurons—specialized cells in our brain—become "overworked" and can no longer coordinate information properly. In this deprived state, we lose our ability to make sound decisions because we're no longer able to accurately assess situations, plan accordingly, and choose the best course of action. There is a reason why the adage "sleep on it" exists. Without sleep, we're just not that good.

For these reasons, I say stop losing sleep over your dreams! You need the freshness of rest daily. But some of you need more than just a good night's rest. You need a solid break. You need to cease work for a season. You need to pause and recover your strength. You'll be hard-pressed to find confidence and courage (which, remember, is an ability) without physical, emotional, and spiritual strength. And you'll be hard-pressed to find strength without allowing all these parts of you to rest and rejuvenate.

Give yourself permission to rest. Commit to getting back out there at the right time—and only you will know that time—but give yourself permission to rest.

REVISIT THE GOALS, REFRESH THE VISION

Nothing in our lives should remain unchanged. Not our hairstyles or our outfit choices or the way we relate to our parents and spouse through the years, and especially not the goals we've set for our lives. The same vision can persist for a lifetime, but goals may need to change. Here's a quick rundown on the difference between the two.

A goal is an observable, measurable outcome you wish to achieve. It's a specific target you want to reach. Losing ten pounds, writing a book, selling a screenplay, starting a business, getting married, and starting a family are all goals. Very commendable goals. But goals without vision are a bunch of random targets.

Vision is your why. Why do you want to lose ten pounds? Why do you want to write a book or screenplay? Why do you want to start a business or a family? Vision is rooted in your core values, your passions, and the calling you believe is on your life. Vision is your higher purpose. Whether it's to live a physically and mentally healthy life or to know true love and to give it back wholeheartedly or to serve people with your talents and gifts or to fully self-actualize and leave this earth emptied, vision is what gives meaning to our lives. The best part about vision is that, while there may be one singular vision in your heart, there are actually innumerable ways to go about achieving it. You can pursue countless goals to manifest your vision.

I once coached someone about her burning desire to start a church. She felt the call of "pastor" on her life and had dreams, prophecies, and years of confirmation to back it up. However, her resources were extremely limited at this particular point in her life, and the people most excited about being served by her ministry were located all over the world. How on earth was she going to do this?

Her growing discouragement caused her to reach out to me. When we met, we distinguished her goal (to start a church) from her vision (to devote her life to shepherding and facilitating healing in God's people). We then brainstormed new goals that would still support her higher purpose but be more within her reach at this particular point in her journey.

I'm happy to share that she is now working a new plan of growing a Facebook community of people who feel led to her leadership and are benefiting from her weekly messages straight from Facebook's live platform. Starting an in-house church may still be in the cards for her, but she doesn't have to wait to fulfill purpose before she finds out.

REFRAME FAILURE AS OPPORTUNITY

"Failure is only the opportunity more intelligently to begin again," Henry Ford once said, and I believe him. I believe him because over one hundred years ago, a young old Henry Ford clocked in at his day job every morning but labored over a gasoline engine every night. The first gas-powered engine had already been created by Carl Benz (yes, *that* Benz), but nobody but the richest of the rich could afford them. Ford had the heart and drive to create a car for the middle class, but this would require more efficient production methods.

The night before Christmas in 1893, Ford got an engine to work for thirty seconds, just long enough to know he was on the right track. Three years later (in 1896) he constructed the Ford Quadricycle, his first model car. Seven years later (in 1903), after a few trial cars and a couple of failed companies, Ford Motor Company was born. Five years after that (in 1908), Ford introduced the Model T, the first car to be affordable for most Americans, making it a huge commercial success. And seven years later (in 1913), Ford launched the first moving assembly line for the mass production of automobiles, which revolutionized the entire industry. One hundred years later Ford Motor Company would grow to become one of the largest and most profitable family-controlled companies in the world.

When failure meets you at your doorstep, pick it up, take it in, and put it in a different frame. Change the story. Try saying to yourself, *This may* feel *like failure, but it's simply an opportunity*. Then have a conversation—either with yourself or with your friends, small group, business partner, or, heck, your mom—about what that opportunity could be. Like Henry Ford, your "failure" could simply be a chance to try something different. Something that will work this time. Or the next time. Or the time after that.

Or maybe the "failure" is an opportunity to grow in problem-solving, financial responsibility, budgeting, or generosity. Or maybe it's an opportunity to be stretched, far and wide, in preparation for the bigger and better things God wants to do next. Or maybe it's an opportunity for something deeper. Maybe the chance to grow in character, patience, faith, persistence, or love. Let me tell you something: it is so freeing to have the emotional agility to be able to easily say "I am sorry" when you've hurt someone unintentionally, to make amends and a commitment to do better, and to quickly move on. But this requires being able to get to a space where you know that failure, even in relationships, isn't something to beat yourself up over; it's an opportunity to learn. Of course, your genuineness and commitment to grow, and their willingness to forgive, are key parts of the equation. But if both parties are willing to meet each other, reconciliation doesn't always have to be so difficult.

Then in the soul-crushing case of being told you can't have children, maybe this is the season that you consider giving an unclaimed child a home. Maybe when that crushing pain lifts but for a second, you'll see a bit of grace in the storm.

GOD WILL REMEMBER YOU

We've yet to talk about my favorite part of Hannah's story, the part found in verses 19-20, which reads:

> Early the next morning they arose and worshiped before the Lord and then went back to their home in Ramah. Elkanah made love to his wife Hannah, and the LORD remembered her. So in the course of time, Hannah became pregnant and gave birth to a son. She named him Samuel, saying, "Because I asked the LORD for him."

The Scripture says the Lord "remembered" Hannah. This is something worth looking at. Did God forget her? Does God forget us? Keep in mind that the Old Testament, where this story is found, was not written in English but in Hebrew. (And the New Testament in Greek.) So, for clarity, we should really be looking at the original Hebrew word used here.

That word is *zakar*. When the Bible says God "remembered," the original Hebrew verb used there is *zakar*. While one definition of zakar is "to remember," another is "to bring someone to mind and then act upon that person's behalf." When you consider the other times God "remembered" someone in the Old Testament (Noah in Genesis 8:1, Rachel in Genesis 30:22, Joseph in Genesis 40:14), it is this second definition that seems more fitting. God didn't just bring these spiritual heroes to mind and think about how nice their personalities were. God acted on their behalf. So it was with Hannah. Elkanah made love to his wife, and God remembered her.

I love how the Scripture describes Hannah and Elkanah's love-making. It is simple and straight to the point. Elkanah made love to his wife. It's almost as if there wasn't anything particularly different, particularly special, or particularly magical about this intimate moment they shared. This is not a knock on their sex life; this is just an observation. Scripture implies that they made love to each other just like they would have any other time of the week. But this time, *this* time, something happened. This time, the Lord had a different answer. This time, the Lord opened Hannah's womb and she became pregnant with her son.

Family, I need you to know that you're not doing anything wrong. You are not broken, God is not broken, and the prophecies over your life still stand. The conscious choices you are making, year after year, to find love in your life, to save your marriage, to lay hold of your calling, and to thrive in your business or career are not in vain. The prayers you're sending up, year after year, are not being ignored. The tears, the anguish, the frustration you face, year after year, just means you're fighting. Hard. And there was never a battle victory without a battle scar.

REAPING A HARVEST

Galatians 6:9 exhorts us: "Let us not become weary in doing good, for at the proper time we will reap a harvest if we do not give up." God is intimately aware of our discouragement but still calls us to keep up our faith. He knows how easy it is to lose hope in what he can do but challenges us to continue in courage. He also promises that at the right time, we will reap a harvest "if we do not give up." Notice that the promise is of something really good—a harvest—but the details of the harvest are left out. This is important.

What I've learned in my own faith journey is that God does indeed honor our faith and courage—however, sometimes not in the way we've imagined it. Sometimes God surprises us. Sometimes God re-calibrates us, and our requests change. Sometimes God invites us to take on a new journey altogether, and when we do so, we experience him and his purposes in even greater ways. No matter what, though, there's a harvest. No matter what, our faith and courage will result in his faithfulness and abundance.

As you work and till the life God has given you, trust that no matter what, something good is coming. Your labor is never in vain.

YEAR NINE

Let's get back to Natalie's story from the beginning of this chapter.

My discouragement-turned-depression took me out of the job hunting for a year because I desperately needed to heal. It was now my eighth year out of school, but I was doing much better. I didn't have my career yet, but I was mentally stronger, spiritually encouraged, and committed to the purpose I knew God had for my life. I kept working to pay my bills.

Then year nine came. Year nine. At the top of the year, I reconnected with an old colleague. She knew people that knew people in—get this—the same organization I had applied to when I first graduated. She told me to send my materials and I did. I had nothing to lose.

Within a week, I was being interviewed via phone by the vice president of the organization. This was getting serious. However, I was still back home, and this position was across the country. I don't know how or why, but faith took over. I moved. I moved before hearing back from the preliminary phone interview. I moved with hope and expectation. It was a good thing I did, because within a week of moving to the city where the job was, I got the call to come in for a follow-up interview, which I knocked out of the park.

Weeks passed by after that interview, but I was so protective over my health and happiness that I didn't even pay attention. I spread my net wide again and took interviews with other bill-paying jobs, just in case. Then I got the call. The call. The position that I'd set my heart on nine years ago but didn't get was officially going to be mine. It'd been fully funded but vacant for a few years because they couldn't find the right person. Looks like it had my name on it all this time.

ENCOURAGEMENT, TENDERNESS, AND LOVE

I have found that one of the most powerful things I can do during a season of discouragement is to wrap myself in encouragement, tenderness, and love. It is the same with my clients, friends, and students. It is likely the same for you. You need encouragement for your discouragement. You need to deal with yourself with tenderness. You need to speak to yourself in love.

Wrapping yourself in encouragement means surrounding yourself with people who will speak life into you. It means finding a community—be it a church, a gym, or a writer's group—that will pursue purpose with you and remind you that you are not alone. It is sitting quietly with a book that brings strength and resolve to your heart. It is collecting cards and notes and texts that you can refer back to privately when everything inside you wants to give up. For me, it's a collection of texts from my mother that I may just create a devotional out of one day. That's how healing they've been to me. Let me share a few of my favorites from over the years because I believe there's a word in them for you too.

Beautiful Peace. Raise your head high. There is nothing wrong with you. There is nothing missing. It is about the timing of the Lord. I love you.

Beautiful Peace. I pray you overcome the enemy's camp and move forward in all your dreams and aspirations. I love you.

Beautiful Peace. You are blessed and highly favored. The Lord is working behind the scenes to bless you. This month will bring good things. I pray the joy of the Lord be your strength. I love you.

Beautiful Peace. Play classical music, sip some ginger tea, and cover yourself with warmth. You are loved.

Great, huh? Stay close to the people who reflect the love, tenderness, and encouragement of God in your life. Be open with them and let them know they are needed. Pray for more of these types of people or experiences in your life if you feel you are lacking. Become this type of person to yourself. And please hear this from me:

> *My Sister, my Brother*
> *You are blessed and highly favored.*
> *The Lord is working behind the scenes to bless you.*
> *This month will bring good things.*
> *May the joy of the Lord be your strength.*
> *With Love, Peace*

ANXIETY

Our Need to Feel Safe

I've spent most of my life and most of my friendships
holding my breath and hoping that when people get close
enough they won't leave, and fearing that it's a matter
of time before they figure me out and go.

SHAUNA NIEQUIST

Chronic anxiety is a state more undesirable than any other,
and we will try almost any maneuver to eliminate it. Modern man
is living in anxious anticipation of destruction. Such anxiety can be
easily eliminated by self-destruction. As a German saying puts
it: "Better an end with terror than a terror without end."

ROBERT E. NEALE

Sometimes you have to dig pretty hard to see
how the anxiety is affecting life or work.

DAVID ROANE

I just give myself permission to suck. . . .
I find this hugely liberating.

JOHN GREEN

Tension is who you think you should be.
Relaxation is who you are.

CHINESE PROVERB

THAINA'S STORY
MY PARENTS' MARRIAGE WAS ENDING
WHILE MINE WAS JUST STARTING

About two years ago, I got married. I remember thinking that I'd waited for marriage to have sex and so I'd "reap my reward." I'd also had a seemingly perfect example of what life in love looked like in my parents. My husband and I would just follow in their path and we'd be thriving in marriage until the end of our days. Then real life happened and cracked my normal. My parents' marriage took a turn for the worst in the most unexpected and sudden way. Here I was starting my own marriage, but theirs was ending. I immediately became more anxious that my husband and I could catch the same fate. It was the first time I had to consider that people do leave.

This complicated my sex life with my husband. I could no longer use abstinence as a shield of protection for our relationship as I had for years prior. But how was I supposed to keep giving myself to a man who could just up and leave me after our kids are grown? I became irritable, restless, and would worry excessively. I was tense during moments of intimacy. Not only was I not prepared to deal with my discomfort with sex after being taught my whole life that sex was "bad," I wasn't prepared to deal with the reality that you could give yourself to someone fully after waiting and have it end in pain. I feared a hypothetical future. Thankfully, my husband was patient. Psychologically, I had so much to unpack.

COLLEEN'S STORY
DATING BROUGHT OUT MY CRAZY

I was single and ready to mingle, but I absolutely hated dating. Hated everything about it. I hated the small talk of first dates, the awkward who's-going-to-pay moment, the uncomfortable realization that one person likes the other more, and even just figuring out where to meet quality people in the first place. But I especially hated what dating did to me. Within a couple weeks of getting involved with a guy I started to like, I would regularly find myself on the verge of panic. If said guy went a full day without calling, by night time I would be so wound up, so tense, I wanted to punch someone. If the guy said one thing that I wasn't sure I liked, I would find myself ruminating on it later until my heart rate shot up, my breathing got short, and I was composing a three-page text about how this relationship wasn't going to work.

I knew things were really off when one morning, a guy who regularly sent me good morning texts didn't do so that day, and by noon I was in tears. I felt absolutely insane and scolded myself for the umpteenth time with the "See, this is why you're still single" trope, which only made me cry harder. But dating brought out my crazy. It was just the truth.

ANXIETY DEFINED

If you were to peek into the *Diagnostic and Statistical Manual of Mental Disorders* (*DSM*)—the handbook used by mental health professionals to officially diagnose mental disorders—you would find a very concise definition of anxiety: the anticipation of future threat. This is certainly not incorrect. But I don't know that it speaks to the core of the experience. Neither does it capture the fullness and variety of what it means to be anxious.

For me, I prefer a more comprehensive definition of anxiety that's still surprisingly simple. More importantly, it gets to the heart of what we all truly feel when we experience it. *Anxiety is what we feel when we don't feel safe.*

Remember, safety is one of our most fundamental needs. Some would argue that after food, water, and air, it's our next most important one. Our need for emotional safety is included in this definition as well. We have just as great a need to feel safe in our relationships as we do in the various situations that we find ourselves in. We don't function well in life or relationships when a feeling of safety is lacking.

During the global pandemic of 2020, anxiety was widespread. Coverage of Covid-19 persisted for months. Grocery shelves looked apocalyptic. People hoarded food and toilet paper. Political tensions rose as people differed greatly on best strategies for moving forward. On a more positive note, loved ones reached out to others to make amends. That's what you do when you confront the uncertainty of the future. Collectively it felt like our safety was on the line and therefore our survival. As a result, fear and anxiety drove our behaviors and changed how we lived.

OUR BODY'S ALARM SYSTEM

Our need for safety isn't dramatic. God set us up to be attracted to safety because our survival would depend on it. It's the reason he created us with an inbuilt alarm system for which we should truly be thankful. Referred to as our fight-or-flight response, this alarm goes off when we appear to be in danger.

Imagine for a second you are walking home alone on a dark night. A growling animal jumps out of a bush and squares off with you. You realize it's a mountain lion. Your body's fight-or-flight response instantly kicks into gear. Your heart beats faster to pump more blood to your muscles because it's time for you to r-u-n. Your eyes dilate to let more light in so you can see your path more clearly. Your lungs expand so you can take in more air as you move with speed. You sweat like crazy to decrease your body temperature and keep your brain cool enough to keep functioning. A host of other physiological changes take place to mobilize your body for action. Then you get home safely and tell Alexa to play "Survivor" by Destiny's Child because you, my friend, most certainly are one.

And you have your fear to thank. It's what kicked everything into gear.

Fear is the sense of unease, doom, or apprehension we feel in response to real or perceived imminent threat. Like in the case of the mountain lion, the threat is distinct and definite. The danger is clear and present. If you were to go home later and tell your family about this, you would have no problem describing the event.

Of course, we're not just afraid of mountain lions. A Chapman University study on American fears showed that among our top fears are public speaking, heights, flying, drowning, blood and needles, bugs, and even clowns.[1] None of these necessarily present any real danger, only perceived. (Well, except clowns—those things are awful!) However the object of fear is clear. Significantly, the specificity of fear makes it easier to treat.

OBJECTLESS FEAR

Now, sometimes this alarm goes off when we're not in immediate danger. Sometimes our bodies respond with fear to a weak signal of threat, an unclear signal, or a signal we don't have yet but we anticipate. These are the conditions for anxiety.

Whereas fear is typically a response to something clear and present, anxiety is a response to something that hasn't happened yet. Whereas fear is a response to something specific, anxiety is typically a response to loosely defined possibilities. Anxiety doesn't wait until something jumps out at you. Anxiety rises at the idea that something could. Sigmund Freud once described anxiety as "objectless fear." You won't always be able to point to something specific, but it's there.

Since there is no imminent threat, anxiety is experienced as more of a nondescript, vague feeling. It's powerful and overwhelming, but ambiguous and free-floating. It's hard to pinpoint the who, what, where, when, and, why of it, making it more challenging to manage and treat.

Emotionally and physiologically, anxiety can feel just like fear. But there is a third component: worry. Worry is the cognitive (thinking) component. Worrying is that constant wondering about a problem or concern, be it specific or diffuse. You can worry about one thing happening or you can worry about one hundred different things happening, and both scenarios can feel pretty intense. Worry often takes the form of "what if" thinking—for example, "What if my relationship fails?" "What if I can't do this?" "What if my children get hurt?" In Thaina's story, she had "what ifs" and worries about her new marriage. With worrying, there's an internal bias that something will go wrong.

Now, worry does have its place. It's a catalyst for problem solving in situations that truly need a solution, such as being short on rent for the month or the approaching date of a career-defining exam. But worry can also become irrational, obsessive, or directed at things beyond our control, and that's when measures need to be taken. We often spend valuable energy worrying about the future.

THE ANXIETY SPECTRUM

Anxiety is a huge umbrella term for lots of different kinds of anxiety-related experiences, including anxiety disorders. I'm in the camp of mental health professionals who like thinking about anxiety as a spectrum experience. Anxiety isn't just a "you've got it or you don't" kind of thing. There are degrees of it. You can find yourself in about a zillion different places on this spectrum experience and still be affected enough to benefit from support.

Think about anxiety as a continuum:

Normal Anxiety → *Almost Clinical Anxiety* → *Clinical Anxiety*

Normal anxiety. On one end of the spectrum, we have normal anxiety. This is the mild to moderate anxiety you might feel right before a job interview, a "we need to talk" conversation, or an exam. This level of anxiety is generally productive, as it helps you prepare seriously for an important task or challenge. Preparation is good. Normal anxiety usually dissipates once the anxiety-producing event is over or behind us. Normal anxiety is commensurate with experience.

Clinical anxiety. On the opposite end of the spectrum, we have clinical anxiety. Clinical anxiety is another umbrella term for anxiety disorders. Disorders describe struggles with anxiety that have begun to overtake someone's life. Specifically, disorders noticeably impair people's ability to function at school, work, or in their daily life. Here are the five different anxiety disorders of adulthood to date:

- *Generalized Anxiety Disorder (GAD).* A chronic, debilitating form of anxiety characterized by excessive, uncontrollable worry about many different things.

- *Social Anxiety Disorder.* An intense fear of being criticized or judged in social or performance situations. The anxiety can be so extreme that it inhibits socializing, dating, and travel.

- *Panic Disorder.* Characterized by recurrent panic attacks. A panic attack is a short, clear-cut period of intense fear, discomfort, and physical symptoms such as rapid heart rate, sweating, difficulty breathing, dizziness, and so on that peak within ten minutes. These attacks create fear about experiencing them again in the future and thus alter one's behavior.

- *Specific Phobia.* An intense fear of a specific object, animal, or nonperformance situation. These objects and situations are avoided at all costs or endured with extreme distress.

- *Agoraphobia.* An intense fear about situations where escape might be difficult or help might not be available if something bad were to happen (e.g., public transportation, open spaces, enclosed spaces, and being outside the home alone).

Remember that with any diagnostic information, it's important to confirm your suspicions about the nature and severity of your symptoms with a licensed mental health professional. Only they are trained to look at subtle nuances and rule out similar but distinct conditions.

Almost clinical. Somewhere in the middle of "normal anxiety" and "clinical anxiety" is a level of anxiety that doesn't quite meet the professional criteria for a particular anxiety disorder but affects your life nonetheless. This is a newer area of research gaining some wind, and I couldn't be happier. In seasons of high anxiety in my life, I would seek out resources and almost be disappointed *not* to find myself in any of the above disorders. It felt somewhat invalidating. If an anxiety disorder didn't account for my distress, then what did? Have any of you ever felt like this?

Then came the work of Dr. Luana Marques, the first I'd seen to officially research, recognize, and professionally acknowledge this middle ground. "Almost anxious" is how she refers to this middle ground. I like using the term "almost clinical" to describe it, as it seems more validating that though symptoms aren't quite clinical, they *almost* are.

HIGH-FUNCTIONING ANXIETY

If I could add one more point to this spectrum, it would be a phenomenon that psychologists have defined informally as high-functioning anxiety. High-functioning anxiety is not an official diagnosis. Instead, it's a phrase used to describe individuals who look like the picture of calm and control while inside managing almost clinical levels of anxiety. If you're an avid watcher of the show *This Is Us*, this is where I would put Randall Pearson if he didn't already meet full criteria for an anxiety disorder.

High-functioning anxiety has characterized some of my mental health journey. I remember a season in my life where everything had to be perfect. To be honest, it wasn't an impossible goal for me. I did well with many things, and the people in my life often affirmed me. "You're so inspiring." "What can't you do?" "You're my role model."

These messages were incredibly flattering, but for someone with a propensity for anxiety, it also mounted the pressure. I couldn't disappoint. I had to be successful. I prided myself on rising early in the mornings, much earlier than most, to get to work on my businesses. I could and would sit at a computer for sixteen hours straight. The anxiety of falling short of expectations would be my "coffee." Sometimes I would work straight through the night.

In my work, which included planning events, I'd do things like create a guest list in the hundreds and contact every single person on the list myself. I had a team, but most things I felt compelled to handle myself. With the guest list, I needed a personal promise to me that they would attend. If they were uncertain, I'd immediately replace them, as the thought of an empty seat created even more anxiety. Overworking every detail, I would cry at times from sheer exhaustion.

While in therapy about this, one of the first memories I recovered was from a childhood birthday party. I'd invited my whole class and was really excited. Then the day came and only three kids showed up. I was devastated. All my family's hard work and money down the drain. I remember even feeling guilty. I realized that my obsession with planning large events and working overtime for them was in some ways about this birthday party. I couldn't fix my past, but I could control my present. Perfectionism was the way I was coping with my fear of rejection.

Individuals with high-functioning anxiety are productive and effective, but deep down they are largely motivated by fears of failure and rejection. This fear is often accompanied by excessive worry, rumination, and procrastination, and sometimes manifests physically in the form of stomachaches, headaches, and slight tremors and shakes. An increased need for reassurance and a closed-off social life (turning down social invitations) may also be a part of the picture.

THE ANXIETY OF INSECURITY

Finally, one more portrait of anxiety you won't find in the *DSM*: insecurity. However, anxiety is exactly what you feel when you're feeling insecure.

In the case of classic anxiety, the threat posed is physical and psychological. In the case of insecurity, the threat is social. There is a fear of not measuring up in the eyes of others and ultimately not being accepted as you are. This is at the heart a fear of rejection, and as you already know, our need to belong is so great that the idea of rejection can feel tragic.

Remember, anxiety is what we feel when we don't feel safe. In the case of insecurity, what doesn't feel secure is our good-enough-ness. We don't feel good enough to try out for the play. We don't feel good enough to author a book. We don't feel good enough to put ourselves out there for a date. We don't feel good enough to capitalize on our skills and start a business. Good enough also comes in the form of pretty enough, attractive enough, smart enough, thin enough, savvy enough, and so on, to gain acceptance into whatever space that we desire to be in. In fact, if we were to try, we'd be laughed away—at least that's what our insecurity tells us—and there is absolutely nothing safe about that.

So, we feel anxious. The same sweaty palms, racing heartbeat, shaking, trembling, and feelings of doom and dread overtake us, keeping us right where we are. Stuck. Sometimes this insecure anxiety is just for a moment. Sometimes it pervades and persists in other parts of our lives. All the time it's uncomfortable and warrants a good look at where it came from.

Research points to a few different sources, one being a critical inner voice. When you experience a wave of insecurity, you are ultimately cued in to a highly critical inner voice. This inner voice is real. So real that the part of our brain responsible for producing speech—Broca's area—shows activity when our inner voice speaks. It's so real that the part of our throat that holds our vocal cords—the larynx—makes small muscular movements when our inner voice talks to us. Our inner voice is so real and so powerful, it's actually insane.

Do you know where a critical inner voice comes from? You probably guessed it: a critical childhood. Somewhere in your childhood, your parents, caregivers, teachers, peers, or even just the culture you grew up in helped you develop an inner voice that saw nothing but fault. Healing your inner voice may require that you begin to speak words of life not only to the adult you are now but to the little child that's still inside you. This is called inner-child work. It's a focus in psychotherapy that helps people get in touch with the unmet needs of childhood and heal the emotions and experiences of childhood that never were.

CLASSIC THEORIES FOR ANXIETY

If you've done any kind of research on your own or have worked with a psychotherapist, you've likely come across these classic theories of the causes of anxiety.

Family history. Research has shown the influence of family background on our development of anxiety in two ways.

- *Genetics.* Studies have consistently shown that anxiety disorders are elevated in children of parents who have anxiety disorders. Studies comparing identical twins (who share 100 percent of their DNA) to fraternal twins (who are no more alike than regular siblings) show increased shared mental health struggles among identical twins. There appears to be a genetic component to anxiety. The genes we came into the world with seem to play a role.

- *Learned behavior.* Fear and anxiety are also learned. If you grew up watching a parent or caregiver respond anxiously to a situation—be it a bug, a rodent, a problem, or just generally in their relationships—that behavior was modeled for you, and your young mind knew nothing else but to download it as a way to be. We don't copy everything our parents do, but we copy a lot.

Past and present trauma. Studies have also confirmed a link between trauma and anxiety. Big-T traumas especially, such as sexual abuse or military combat, appear to increase your risk of developing an anxiety disorder. Little-t traumas, such as bullying and divorce, show links as well. Moreover, the earlier in life these traumas occurred, the more likely it is that it altered your central nervous system in a way that made you more susceptible.

Life stress. We can't underestimate the power of stress in our lives. Stressful life events have also been found to trigger anxiety troubles. Common triggers include, but are not limited to, work stress or job loss, home loss or moving, marital or family discord, financial strain or duress, and even the beautiful miracle of pregnancy and childbirth.

Personality. Personality is a little less talked about, but research suggests that people with certain temperaments or personality traits are more likely to experience anxiety. For example, children and adults who are prone to perfectionism, have a strong need to control everything, are sensitive, highly reactive, and easily flustered, or fit the criteria of a type A personality are most likely to have higher levels of anxiety.

Now, hear me when I say this: trauma, personality, or family history of anxiety is not a sentence for anxiety. It doesn't make your struggle inevitable. Nor does it mean that if you do develop a real problem with it, you will struggle endlessly. Tracing your mental struggles back to their potential causes is meant to empower you. The more you know, the more proactive and focused you can be with your mental health.

A LESS CLASSIC THEORY: A SHIFT IN VALUES

Now for the less classic theories (meaning the theories that haven't been heavily researched yet but probably should be). Psychologists are already having the conversation with their clients and ministers with their churches. Something about the nature of our anxiety collectively feels cultural and spiritual.

In 2017, the American Psychiatric Association (APA) polled one thousand US adults and found that nearly two-thirds were "extremely or somewhat anxious about health and safety for themselves and their families," and more than one-third were more anxious overall than the previous year.[2] By generation, millennials were the most anxious and baby boomers the least. Interestingly, men and women were equally anxious, though we've been led to believe differently, and people of color reported higher levels of anxiety than White people.

In 2018, the APA repeated the same poll and found that anxiety hasn't gone anywhere. In fact, it just increased. And still, millennials suffered the most.

Such findings beg the question: Is our culture at fault? Is the United States breeding more anxiety? If so, how?

With a question this big, we have to acknowledge that there are likely many different answers. Many different considerations and different directions to take. However, we can't deny that something is going on, and it's worth us taking a look. The research just has to catch up and clarify our concerns. Here are two major considerations that have come to light.

One 1996 study conducted by Tim Kasser and Richard M. Ryan found that well-being may be linked to the kinds of goals we have for our lives.[3] Specifically, in a sample of adults, researchers found that extrinsic goals of financial success, good looks, and social recognition were associated with lower vitality, lower self-actualization, and greater physical symptoms. Conversely, the more these adults focused on intrinsic goals like self-acceptance, connection, sense of community, and improving physical health, the better their well-being and stress levels.

Kasser further shed light on these findings in a 2014 interview with the American Psychological Association, where he framed the problem we're having in our culture as a problem with materialism:

> To be materialistic means to have values that put relatively high priority on making a lot of money and having many possessions, as well as on image and popularity. . . . Research shows [that] people are more materialistic when they are exposed to messages that suggest such pursuits are important, whether through their parents and friends, society, or media. Second, and somewhat less obvious—people are more materialistic when they feel insecure or threatened, whether because of rejection, economic fears or thoughts of their own death.[4]

While culture may not be creating our problem with materialism, it surely is capitalizing on it. Between the subtle and not so subtle messaging of media and entertainment, celebrity influence, and social media we're exposed to, how can someone *not* walk away with the idea that the key to happiness is getting more, looking different, and being more popular? I can't remember the last time I heard a message calling me to contentment, inner growth, and service to the community as opposed to making it my audience. Who wouldn't be made existentially anxious by the subtle message that who you are and where you are in your life isn't enough?

I think no one.

THE WISDOM OF ANXIETY

The beauty—yes, beauty—of anxiety is that there is wisdom in it. Anxiety itself counsels and directs. It points back to our families and how we may have learned our fears and anxiety. It points back to our traumas and unhealed wounds. It points back to losses we still need to deal with, whether it be lost life, lost love, or lost time. It points back to values that may have shifted for the culture that just won't work for us. And how could they? These values aren't ones that God made important for our lives.

Anxiety bubbles at the surface with a message from deep down. We should remain curious about it. We should listen. Here are at least three questions you can ask yourself as you listen to your anxiety.

Are you in danger? Because fear and anxiety are ultimately supposed to protect us, we most certainly should take the time to assess if we're in any real danger. If your anxiety suggests that you might be, you must pay attention and take action. I think about the case of someone who just left a relationship characterized by poor boundaries, intimidation, and other signs of abuse. This person may be anxious that their ex could return to their life unexpectedly and somehow hurt them. There's a legitimate threat here that should be worked out with a therapist who specializes in partner violence, and possibly the legal system. The same goes for danger that isn't physical but rather emotional or psychological. Maybe there are friends in your life who are causing more harm than good. Maybe your significant other's drinking is getting a little bit out of control. Maybe the class you're about to do a presentation for is full of sophisticated bullies and you would prefer not to be terrorized just to get a grade. All of these scenarios warrant a bit of your attention, a ton of emotional support, and a reasonable plan for how you want to move forward.

In Thaina's story, the "danger" that confronted her from the beginning was the potential failure of her new marriage, triggered by what had happened with her parents. I imagine it like watching a four-car collision spiral out in front of you, leaving you with a sense that this could have been you too. In either case, you could keep replaying the nightmare in your head, which, by the way, is a defining characteristic of worry. Or you could entertain the possibilities just long enough to put together a plan of protection and then return to the present. After all, that's where your life is. Fortunately, this is what Thaina and her husband ultimately did.

What are my current thoughts? Anxiety typically points to some specific worries. Oftentimes, those worries take the form of "what if?"

- What if they don't like me?

- What if I put myself out there and they reject me?

- What if this ruins our friendship?

- What if she doesn't forgive me?

- What if I fail at this and have to start over again?

- What if this doesn't work out for me?

- What if I take my shot and miss?

- What if, what if, what if?

When anxiety points back to a problem with a bunch of "what ifs," try answering back with the equally powerful question, "So what?" This is a method I picked up from anxiety expert psychologist Dr. Angela Neal-Barnett, who shared about it in her book *Soothe Your Nerves*.[5] "So what" questioning helps anxious individuals realize that what they are fearing could happen is far worse than what might actually happen. Look at some examples for how this works:

- What if they don't like me? (So what?)

- What if I put myself out there and they reject me? (So what?)

- What if this strains our friendship? (So what?)

- What if I fail at this and have to start over again? (So what?)

See, once "what ifs" are met with "so whats," worries begin to shrink in size and significance. Perhaps what's most helpful is the fact that the solutions to our worries become more clear, focused, and executable. For example, if you "so what" your fear about failing and having to start over again, you could work on a plan of action should that actually happen. You would likely also gain some confidence that if this were the outcome, you would survive it.

Is there something unresolved in me? Anxiety acts as a defense mechanism. It often works to protect us from deeper, harder, more uncomfortable emotions until we have the time, space, and support to really deal with them. That being said, your growing anxiety may be a sign that it's time to finally dig in. As you reflect on your recent history, what other feelings keep coming up for you? Is it sadness, bitterness, frustration, shame? Where might these feelings be coming from? Does any current frustration resemble frustration from your past? Are core beliefs being triggered?

Remember Colleen, who felt like dating "brought out the crazy" in her? For her, there were real feelings of insecurity covering up real fears of being abandoned. There were thoughts and core beliefs being uprooted about her ability to be loved. All of her feelings and beliefs worked together like ingredients in a bottle of Coke. Dating was the event that shook the bottle up. When the reassurance she needed didn't come in the exact way she wanted—the good morning text— she imploded. Her anxiety spilled over and took over her decisions.

The wisdom of your anxiety may allude to the fact that anxiety isn't your problem at all. It may be old memories, long-standing insecurities, or deep doubts. These types of issues are best worked out in therapy.

A RELIEVING REGIMEN

It behooves us to remain curious about our anxiety, to listen to it, and to see the path it might want to take us down. However, sometimes anxiety rises, and we just need to relieve it. Sometimes we just need something to get us through the day. Research emphatically supports the use of deep breathing (sometimes called diaphragmatic breathing, belly breathing, or paced breathing), imagery, and meditation to relieve rising levels of anxiety. I've also found it comforting to learn that faithful Christians have practiced things like deep breathing and breath prayer, contemplative prayer, and meditation for centuries!

Deep breathing. Deep breathing is one of the most powerful things you can do for your anxious body. When you slow down and deepen your breath, you send a message to your brain to calm down and relax. You tap into your sympathetic nervous system—the system that controls your fight-or-flight response, which your anxiety reveals has been triggered—and you signal to this system that it's okay to relax. Your brain copies this message and signals to the rest of your body that it can chill. Nine times out of ten, it will.

Breathing exercises are quick, easy, and require nothing of you but a couple of minutes. There are lots of different exercises out there, but one of my favorites is the 4-7-8 method, championed by Dr. Andrew Weil. It's so simple that you can do it whenever and wherever you are. Here are the steps:

1. Breathe in through the nose for 4 seconds.

2. Hold your breath for 7 seconds.

3. Exhale powerfully for 8 seconds.

4. Repeat this 4-5 times.

The power of this exercise is really the emphasis on exhaling. The feeling of "I can't catch my breath" isn't because you're not breathing; it's because you're not exhaling, and that's where the shift happens.

Imagery. Imagery (sometimes called guided imagery) involves the use of your imagination. Let's hope things haven't gotten that bad and we all still have one of those! The idea is that during an anxiety rise, you turn inward and visualize that you are in a much more peaceful place—a quiet beach with gentle waves, a warm fireplace, your grandma's sweet-smelling kitchen in the morning. It doesn't matter what you choose. What matters is that it's a place you can easily see, hear, and smell, and that it's a place in real life that has made you feel safe and calm.

To do this exercise:

1. Find a quiet place, as free from distraction as possible, and settle into a comfortable position.

2. Close your eyes and spend one to two minutes taking those slow, deep breaths. Remember to exhale.

3. Once you're calm, transport yourself, via imagination, to your safe place. Picture it in as much detail as possible. Engage the rest of your senses. What do you hear, taste, and smell? What do you feel on your skin? Stay in this scene for as long as you need or as long as you like.

4. When you're ready, slowly count backward from ten and open your eyes. Notice how you feel. Try and stay in this calm state for the rest of the hour and for as long as you can in your day.

Meditation. Despite the complicated definitions that exist for it, meditation at its core is pure and simple. *Psychology Today* defines meditation as "the practice of turning one's attention to a single point of reference. It can involve focusing on the breath, on bodily sensations, or on a word or phrase, known as a mantra. [It is] pivoting away from distracting thoughts and focusing on the present moment."[6]

When you choose one point of focus and shift your attention from everything else going on around you to that thing, you are meditating. Your meditation may not be very transformative—you could have chosen to meditate on a pencil for all I know—but if you are focused singly on the pencil for any number of minutes, in any place you choose, you are meditating.

May I suggest to you that this is exactly what the Word inspires us to do. Check out these Scriptures:

My eyes stay open through the watches of the night,
    that I may meditate on your promises. (Psalm 119:148)

You will keep in perfect peace
    Those whose minds are steadfast,
        because they trust in you. (Isaiah 26:3)

Be still, and know that I am God;

    I will be exalted among the nations,

    I will be exalted in the earth. (Psalm 46:10)

Finally, brothers and sisters, whatever is true, whatever is noble, whatever is right, whatever is pure, whatever is lovely, whatever is admirable—if anything is excellent or praiseworthy—think about such things. (Philippians 4:8)

Scripture encourages us to turn our attention to a single focus in our anxiety, whether it be God, his promises, or anything that is true, pure, and lovely. This is meditation.

I encourage you to develop your own anxiety regimen or meditation practice that you can fall back on. One you can use alone in your room or together with your church small group or circle of friends. Do more research if you need to (there are tons of books, articles, and practice exercises out there), but keep it pure, keep it simple, and make it work for you. No matter how hard it gets, keep at least one thing in mind: you're not in this alone.

RETURNING TO CALM

Let's return to the stories of Thaina and Colleen. How did they learn to calm their anxiety and worry?

From Thaina, who worried that her parents' fate would be her own fate:

Over time, I learned more about what led to my parents' divorce. As tough as it was, I allowed it to teach me what works in marriage and what doesn't. More importantly, I've learned to surrender our marital journey, trust God with our hearts, and stay in the present. I've learned that daily I must let go of the unknown and just focus on our now. There is so much out of my control, and that's okay. In fact, this is what I remind myself of often: "It's okay. I'm okay. We will be okay." My only focus now is to bring my best to the table. Time has passed, and I'm now no longer concerned about my marriage ending. But this battle has kept me on a journey of continuing to evolve as a woman, wife, and child of God. I'm better for it.

From Colleen, who found her anxiety rising when her phone didn't ring:

I was grateful that morning for already having a soothing regimen I could turn to—calm worship music, journaling, a prayer for peace—but I was really glad I remembered I also had a book nearby with some really good stuff about anxiety. I opened it and turned to the exercise that had me write down my thoughts, feelings, and behaviors. I was able to trace my nervous feelings and self-sabotaging behaviors back to my insecurity. I guess I still doubted someone could really ever want to be with me.

This realization motivated me to turn to my favorite psalm—Psalm 139—which reminded me that I'm "fearfully and wonderfully made." I read this part of the psalm back to myself like it was God himself speaking to me: "Colleen, you are fearfully and wonderfully made." I read it over and over until I believed it.

SADNESS AND DEPRESSION

Our Need for Healthy Thinking, Connection, and Meaning

*Depression is feeling like you've lost something
but having no clue when or where you last had it. Then
one day you realize what you lost is yourself.*

ANONYMOUS

*That's the thing about depression: A human being can survive
almost anything, as long as she sees the end in sight. But depression
is so insidious—and it compounds daily—making it impossible
to ever see the end. That fog is like a cage without a key.*

ELIZABETH WURTZEL

*I don't want to see anyone. I lie in the bedroom with
the curtains drawn and nothingness washing over me like
a sluggish wave. Whatever is happening to me is my own fault.
I have done something wrong, something so huge I can't even
see it, something that's drowning me. I am inadequate
and stupid, without worth. I might as well be dead.*

MARGARET ATWOOD, CAT'S EYE

The sun stopped shining for me is all. The whole story
is: I am sad. I am sad all the time and the sadness is so
heavy that I can't get away from it. Not ever.

NINA LaCOUR, *HOLD STILL*

Losing your life is not the worst thing that can happen.
The worst thing is to lose your reason for living.

JO NESBØ

Depression steals people.

UNKNOWN

JOY'S STORY
THE BAD THOUGHTS CAME IN THE MORNING

The guy I was dating ended things with me . . . on my birthday. Just a few months prior, I watched the guy I fell for before him just up and get married. What had felt so significant between us suddenly felt like it meant nothing. Things were not going well in the love department. They weren't going well at work either. My job was making me miserable, and it was becoming unbearable. I felt unimportant, undervalued, and had lost all joy in it. I had worked and prayed hard for everything in my life, so this was confusing. I didn't know how to deal with any of it, so I didn't. In true "me" form, I just smiled and laughed along with everyone. Life is all about moving forward, right?

Then one night during a drive home, an awful, horrible thought popped into my head randomly. I gripped the steering wheel in horror. This thought was very unlike me. Where did this come from? I ruminated for several long minutes. When I finally got home, I ran into my room, grabbed my Bible, blasted worship music, and prayed. I resolved to forget the thought and move on. I consoled myself by saying, "We all get weird, random thoughts." I was sure this was the last of it.

It was not the last of it. The bad thoughts came the next morning and with each passing day. I began to entertain them: What would happen if I stepped out in front of these cars? I'd for sure die, right? Could I at least induce a coma? My internal world created a storm. I lost my appetite completely. I struggled to sleep. Problems with diarrhea came out of nowhere and further emptied my already shrinking stomach. I was already a petite girl but was quickly losing weight. I started avoiding public places. I think I feared that if I didn't stay home, the bad thoughts would actualize out there somewhere. I would end my life. I withdrew from everyone.

THE FIGHT FOR YOUR LIFE

I'm going to cut straight to the point. A fight with depression is a fight for your life. Depression puts you at great risk for voluntarily giving up the breath that God gave you. It is one condition that, unchecked, will have you seduced by death. This is our spiritual enemy's wish. We surely don't know our last days or what will bring them. And we don't know who gets to stay here or whose time it is to go. But we have to know that for as long as God and life will allow, there is something here for us. We can't let the enemy rob us clean of joy, happiness, and purpose.

I'm so thankful for Joy's story. The irony of a woman of strong faith, fighting to hold on to what she bears by name. Depression is a perplexing reality. Perhaps even more perplexing for the person who has claims to freedom in faith. In a sense, two wars must be waged—one to gain peace in your life and the other to keep your faith.

Whatever the case, to wage any war, we have to get clear on what we're fighting. We need a clear picture of what depression is and what it isn't. We need to honor the emotions God gave us to connect meaningfully to ourselves and each other while remaining vigilant against the dysfunction that doesn't come from him. But before unpacking depression, let's look at its cousins, sadness and grief.

MAKING ROOM FOR SADNESS

As a culture, we are obsessed with happiness. Everywhere you look are books, podcasts, courses, and products designed to make you happier. Happier within yourself and happier in your relationships. Happier in your job and happier in your everyday life. It seems happiness is one of our most important personal goals, and there is nothing wrong with this. Happiness is a beautiful, wonderful, healthy thing.

But so is sadness. The pressure we put on ourselves to be happy all the time is not only unrealistic, it's unhealthy. Emotional range is a hallmark of wellness. The ability to feel and express sadness is important and necessary. Allowing ourselves to feel sadness is actually what helps us to release it. Sadness is a reminder that we are humans with hearts.

Sadness is what we feel when we lose someone or something important to us. It's what we feel when something we value is gone. Common triggers for sadness include

- saying goodbye

- the end of a romantic relationship

- the end of a friendship

- being left out or excluded

- moving, and other life changes or transitions

- the end of a life chapter (e.g., graduation)

- mild disappointments

- global disasters and crises

- certain deaths

Sadness signals to us that we need some soothing and comforting. We need to take some time for recovery. We need support from others and we need to practice self-care. Sadness is also what we feel in response to a loved one's distress. For example, when family, friends, and other people we care for lose something important to them. In this case our sadness signals that it's time to be there for them. Your loving presence, listening ears, words of sympathy, offers to help, and sympathy cards and gifts are needed and appropriate.

The gift of sadness is that it slows us down and inspires reflection. It reveals what's most important in our lives and what gives us meaning. It shows us the things in our lives that are worth fighting for or protecting—be it ourselves, another person, a value, or a dream. It reveals what truly makes us happy. For this reason, it's important to make room for sadness and to listen to what it's trying to tell us:

- Do we need to love a little harder? Do we need to say it more?

- Do we need to show more gratitude or appreciation?

- Do we need to start standing up for ourselves? Do we need to leave a friendship or relationship?

- Do we need to embrace and celebrate the present more since things can change in an instant?

Your sadness will probably tell you. Furthermore, though ordinary sadness will vary somewhat in intensity, a defining characteristic is that it will resolve itself quickly. Especially after you've received and acted on the message it's trying to send. This is one of the many things that distinguishes it from depression.

EXPERIENCING GRIEF

Compared to ordinary sadness, grief ups the ante. While sadness is emotionally uncomfortable, grief feels more like emotional suffering. Grief includes a feeling of deep sadness, but the experience is accompanied by a host of other reactions and symptoms.

Grief is what we often feel in response to bereavement. *Bereavement* is the technical term for a state of deprivation we are in due to the death of a person we love. Death—especially a sudden, untimely one—is crushing, mind-defying, and time-stopping, and can feel like a collapse of reality. Like Seyi, who shared how she suddenly lost her mom to cancer in a previous chapter, death can also leave you feeling wounded and abandoned by God.

But grief can occur after other deep losses as well. Like after the end of a marriage. Or after a life-altering injury or diagnosis. Or after the loss of a dream, big opportunity, or career.

The loss of a piece of one's identity can also lead to grief. I knew someone once who had the brightest athletic future ahead of him. When he was out of high school, expectations were high as scouts tracked him down from all over the country. He was "NFL bound," and coaches and the people of his community were ecstatic. But as soon as he got onto the college field, serious injuries hampered him, one after the other. One year, he could barely even stand up straight, let alone play. He never got the chance to show who he could be on the field. There was no NFL, and it wasn't even a fair fight. He grieved the loss of his dream for years. Who could blame him? As painful as it is, grief is an important process. A process that should be embraced and understood.

The myth of the stages. Perhaps you've come across the work of Elisabeth Kübler-Ross before. She's the death-and-dying expert who identified five "stages" of grief—denial, anger, bargaining, depression, and acceptance. She has single-handedly transformed how much of the world understands death. What you may not know, however, is that her original intent was to develop a framework for understanding how terminally ill patients come to terms with their irreversible illnesses. Still, the world ran away with her ideas and overapplied them to grieving death and other losses, all of it a likely attempt to make a complicated, often overwhelming process seem predictable and manageable.

But grief is not predictable. And studies of people in their grief have shown that it does not follow these nicely defined stages. Those of you who've experienced grief are probably nodding in agreement. What's truer is that there are as many ways to grieve as there are grievers. Every person and story is different. Even Kübler-Ross, in her last book before her death, said of her five stages: "They were never meant to help tuck messy emotions into neat packages. They are responses to loss that many people have, but there is not a typical response to loss, as there is no typical loss. Our grieving is as individual as our lives."[1]

Reactions to grief. Grief doesn't occur in five stages, but there are common symptoms. There are physical, mental, emotional, and spiritual effects that may emerge that will vary from person to person. These reactions may fade one day and return the next. They may circle back again and again. Remember, any or all of this is normal. Also remember these symptoms can occur in response to bereavement or other deep losses. Table 7.1 provides a nonexhaustive list of common reactions to grief.

MOVING THROUGH GRIEF

Like ordinary sadness, grief is a normal response to loss. But unlike ordinary sadness, grief may take real time and space to resolve. Your grief may also require you do some deeper emotional or spiritual work, or that you open yourself up to the assistance of a therapist, counselor, spiritual leader, or small group. Whatever your grief needs, give it permission to tell you. Then as you move through it, keep these few things in mind.

Don't judge your grief. On January 26, 2020, the world grieved the sudden death of legendary basketball player Kobe Bryant. He died in a helicopter crash that also claimed the life of his thirteen-year-old daughter Gianna and seven others.

I remember the exact moment I learned of the news. I was driving home from a manicure and saw my brother's text alert on my phone: "Kobe Bryant is dead." Wait, what? I immediately pulled over to process what I just read. I took to Twitter, and there it was. His tragic death was confirmed. All I could do was scream. Not Kobe Bryant, man. Not

Table 7.1

COMMON REACTIONS TO GRIEF

Emotional Reactions to Grief

- Anger
- Anxiety
- Apathy
- Betrayal
- Denial or disbelief
- Despair
- Fear
- Guilt
- Helplessness
- Loneliness
- Numbness
- Powerlessness
- Rage
- Sadness
- Yearning

Mental Reactions to Grief

- Difficulty concentrating
- Rumination about the loss
- Preoccupation and forgetfulness
- Mental confusion
- Difficulty remembering or gaps in memory
- Increased dreams or nightmares
- "Searching behavior"—looking for the loved one in different places even though you know they're gone
- Self-destructive thoughts

Physical Reactions to Grief

- Oversleeping or difficulty sleeping
- Overeating or undereating
- Tiredness or fatigue
- Headaches and stomachaches
- Heart racing
- Muscle tension
- Feeling weak

Spiritual Reactions to Grief

- Feeling lost or empty
- Feeling wounded or abandoned by God
- Feeling angry with God
- Questioning your beliefs
- Temporary or permanent loss of faith
- Increased spirituality
- Finding new meaning or purpose in life

Common Behaviors

- Fits of crying
- Overachieving or underachieving
- Changes in work or school performance
- Clumsiness and uncoordination
- Withdrawal and wanting to be alone
- Dropping out of activities
- Increased aggression or argumentativeness
- Showing more creative expression

Source: crossroadhospice.com

our Kobe! It felt so unreal. More texts came in from friends. Everybody was sharing their shock and their tears. For a moment, I questioned whether we were feeling too much. None of us knew Kobe personally. Was this our grief to bear?

But when my college students streamed into class the next morning, slowly, solemnly, and heads hung low, I knew that grief was the right way to describe it. This was collective grief. Community grief. Kobe's life meant something to all of us. And so now his death. I devoted my classes that day to honoring the life of our shared hero and honoring the grief that we felt.

Sometimes your grief may surprise you. You may be taken aback by what you're feeling, by how much you're feeling it, and by who or what you're feeling it for. You may be shocked by how deep and wide your feelings go. But know that a loss will take on different meanings for different people, and nobody has the right to tell another how to feel. Whatever the cause, if the signs of grief are there, allow yourself time to feel and move through it. Honor your process with space, time, self-compassion, and self-care.

Don't rush your grief. There is also no set timetable for grieving. Some grief lessens after a few days or weeks. Some grief takes months and years. Some grief will come in waves over time. Some grief will lay dormant then peak in a whole new, otherwise happy season. Different factors are at play here, including one's personality, natural coping style, faith, beliefs, expectations, support system, and of course how significant the loss was to a person. There is no normal timeline for grieving—there is just the time you need.

Don't force your grief. Sometimes there is no catastrophic feeling in the face of bereavement. Maybe the feelings haven't fully hit you yet, or maybe you're still in a bit of denial. Which, by the way, is okay since sometimes the brain needs a little time to take it all in.

Trauma psychologist Ronnie Janoff-Bulman says moderate denial in the face of death is the brain's way of "dosing" itself.[2] Fully accepting the death of the loved one is necessary at some point. But too much reality too quickly can add more pain than is necessary at a given moment. Grief can also be complicated because the relationship with the person you lost was complicated. Or maybe your grief process isn't like anybody else's. Maybe you won't cry ever next to another family member who won't stop. In times of deep loss, you will have to get to know your grief. Embrace it. No one gets to make sweeping statements about the nature and quality of your grief. Nor do they get to question your love. When it comes to grief, do what feels right for you—provided it's not destructive—and then just keep doing it until you no longer need to.

BEYOND SADNESS AND GRIEF

You'll notice soon that some of the symptoms of sadness and grief overlap with symptoms of depression. So how do we know the difference? For one, sadness and grief naturally dissipate over time. Depression is far more aggressive, persistent, and pervasive. Sadness and grief are normal responses to loss. Depression can begin with loss and spiral into something deeper, or it can start without any such connection to loss or bereavement. Sadness and grief are often focused on the loss or an external circumstance. Depression's focus is usually inward and causes feelings of worthlessness, guilt, and self-doubt. With grief, it may feel like you're at war with God or the world. With depression, your war is within yourself.

Similar to anxiety, depression is an umbrella term for its different flavors. Sometimes the word is used to describe the everyday "depression" that we'll say we feel during hardship or after some type of loss. Other times it's used to describe clinically significant depression that points to the need for professional attention. This certainly can make things confusing. Here's a snapshot of some of the most common types of depression.

Major Depressive Disorder (MDD). MDD is a serious mental illness that negatively impacts how you think, feel, and behave. It's usually the kind of depression professionals reference when the term "clinical depression" is used. The primary characteristics are persistent feelings of sadness and/or a loss of interest in activities that one once enjoyed, accompanied by some of the following other symptoms:

- changes in appetite—loss of appetite or eating too much
- changes in sleeping—difficulty sleeping or sleeping too much
- loss of energy or increased fatigue
- slowed movements and speech or increase in purposeless activity (e.g., hand-wringing or pacing)
- feeling worthless or guilty
- difficulty thinking or concentrating
- thoughts of death or suicide

Persistent Depressive Disorder (PDD). Once known as dysthymia, PDD is characterized by depression that is present for at least two years. The symptoms may not be as severe as that of major depressive disorder, but they are persistent and pervasive.

Bipolar Disorder. Bipolar disorder is characterized by periods of major depression interspersed with episodes of mania. A manic episode refers to a period of at least one week of elevated mood, racing thoughts, decreased need for sleep, increased goal-directed activity, excessive involvement in pleasurable activities (e.g., shopping sprees or hypersexuality), and inflated self-esteem.

Seasonal Affective Disorder (SAD). SAD, now called major depressive disorder with "seasonal pattern," refers to symptoms of depression that emerge during winter months but subside in the spring.

Postpartum Depression (PPD). Officially called depression with "peripartum onset," PPD is brought about by the significant hormonal shifts that accompany pregnancy. The onset of PPD can occur during pregnancy or just following the birth of the child, and its symptoms typically include feelings of sadness, anxiety, mood swings, withdrawal, feelings of worthlessness and inadequacy, and trouble bonding with your baby. Perhaps most distressing are thoughts of suicide during this time, or thoughts of hurting yourself or even your baby. It's all part of the depression.

Atypical Depression. Officially called depressive disorder with "atypical features," atypical depression is characterized by common symptoms of depression—including excessive eating, excessive sleep, and fatigue—alongside intense sensitivity to rejection and highly reactive moods. Distinctively, this depression appears to lift in the face of a positive event.

To be given any diagnosis, symptoms must persist for a certain amount of time (which varies according to type), negatively impact or impair one's daily life, or be highly distressing. By now, it should go without saying that any curiosities about meeting criteria for a diagnosis should be discussed with a licensed mental health professional. Clinically significant depression is serious, and working with a trained professional could mean the difference between life and death.

A NOTE ON SUICIDE:
THE REALITY AND THE MYTHS

Every year at an annual campus wellness event, I ask my students to close their eyes and answer the question: "Who in here has ever thought about suicide?"

I work at a Christian university with many students from "good" families—all with incredible potential for success. Guess how many of them raise their hands?

Almost every single one.

I used to be really caught off guard by this. Despite my expertise, I would look on with disbelief, doubting whether these students actually heard me correctly. I wasn't prepared to see the hands slowly rise, becoming more plentiful than the hands that didn't, as if I'd asked about a food preference or a common schoolyard experience.

But now, I take it with stride. My heart still breaks with the truth about depression, but at least I'm clear on the reality of what we're dealing with. We are struggling collectively with a reason to keep living. We are struggling collectively with the conviction for life. The things I'd previously believed about suicide were folklore. It was now my responsibility to expose the myths. Here are a few of them.

Suicide myth #1: suicide is rare. Suicide is the second leading cause of death among American individuals ages ten to thirty-four, and the fourth leading cause of death among individuals thirty-five to fifty-four, according to a 2017 CDC report. The same report showed that there were twice as many suicides as there were homicides that year. Additionally, for every one "successful" suicide, it is estimated that up to twelve people have at least tried to. Suicide is not rare; it is happening every day, all around us.

Suicide myth #2: suicide happens to weak people. There's this misconception that the people who die by suicide are those timid, weak, withdrawn individuals in the corner who take up very little space and pretty much go unheard. While the withdrawn and isolated show warning signs for suicide, countless people who consider, attempt, or successfully complete it are highly impactful, successful, goal-driven women and men. Maybe not so surprising is the fact that many of them are great at helping other people but pros at masking their own pain. They are the strong ones in people's lives. But who do the strong ones turn to for help?

Suicide myth #3: people who die by suicide want to die. Most people thinking about suicide do not want to die. They want to live, but they just want to stop hurting. They want to be in control again—of their thoughts, of their painful emotions, and of their experiences and environment—but they just don't know how. They will do most anything to regain that control. For some that leads to the decision to end their life. It's thought that the idea feels empowering to some—like it's a final way to resume control, even if death is the result.

Suicide myth #4: suicide is selfish. It's understandable to think this way about suicide, considering the loved ones left behind. But consider another perspective. Individuals thinking about suicide often feel that "everybody would be better off" without them. In fact, they might be doing their loved ones a favor. It's important to realize that this may be a theme in someone's thinking pattern, and if you're ever in a position to hear someone go down this path, go ahead and call it out for what it is—a lie!

Suicide myth #5: suicide doesn't happen to the praying Christian. In 2019 I knew people deeply affected by the decision of their pastors to take their own life. Jarrid Wilson, a thirty-year-old pastor of a Southern California megachurch and founder of a mental health advocacy group, was found dead the same night he earlier tweeted: "Loving Jesus doesn't always cure suicidal thoughts. Loving Jesus doesn't always cure depression."

It's chilling.

His death followed the suicide of Andrew Stoecklein, another thirty-year-old pastor of a popular church in Southern California, who took his life just days after preaching about his own mental health struggles. These were just a few young guys in my neck of the woods. A few guys who loved and were led by Jesus. A few guys who happened to be well-known enough to make waves in the headlines. How many more are out there who won't make the news?

The grip of suicidal thinking isn't reserved for the quiet, withdrawn, or faithless. It isn't a self-centered, one-off decision. It's a symptom of deep struggle that is depression, and it can knock on any one of our hearts. When it comes to dealing with suicidal thinking, it's best we lead with compassionate curiosity, openness to understanding, and grace. Even if the object of concern is ourselves.

THE DEEPER REASONS WHY

Despite some controversy in the medical community, our culture has rallied around the idea that too little or too much of a certain brain chemical is solely to blame for the onset of a depressive disorder. While brain chemicals certainly do play a role in mood and disorder, the picture is far more complex. One tip-off is the fact that antidepressants—expertly targeted to restore chemical balance—only work in about 50 percent of cases. This is telling. For about 50 percent of cases, we've been misfiring. Something else is going on, and it's time we look at it squarely in the face.

Reason #1: broken thinking, broken brain. Early in my students' academic journey, they learn about the plasticity of the brain. That is, they learn that throughout our lives the brain can change. I have fun showing them clips of six-month-olds who can tell the difference between identical looking primates but then lose that ability by the time they're nine months. Since human babies don't need the super skill of distinguishing primates from one another, but rather the ability to distinguish their human caregivers from strangers, the latter skill is what will be strengthened throughout their early years.

Unused abilities will disappear. It's the repetition of their actual experiences that matters here. That's what the brain wraps itself around. Experience. Experience acts like an architectural blueprint for a developing brain.

Thought itself is also an experience. This has been the focus of Dr. Caroline Leaf, a cognitive neuroscientist and a believer who studies, among other things, the mind-brain connection. Her work has revealed the incredible discovery that thought itself changes the brain. Our thinking can literally alter brain structure and matter. It's mind-blowing.[3] (Pun intended.)

In the case of depression, one of the things that appears to be happening is that our past traumas still live inside of us. Add to that our current dramas, unexpected crises, and overwhelming stress, and it's enough to feel like giving up. Who could blame us? We can all be validated by Allen Barbour, an internist at Stanford University, who once said, "Depression isn't a disease; depression is a normal response to abnormal life experiences."[4]

Still, the reality of the situation is that our minds work to create a story about what happened to us. Our minds ultimately assess, evaluate, interpret, and internalize these abnormal experiences and weave them into the brain like a pattern. They continue to do this throughout adulthood, traumas or not. Our minds have the final word.

So, in the case of depression, you can think about it like this: when bad things happen in our lives, our thoughts about them create a particular brain environment. Bad thinking creates bad brain biochemistry. Toxic thinking creates toxic brain chemistry. Broken thinking creates a broken brain. A chemical imbalance will certainly sustain our depression, but it's possible that our thoughts play the bigger role in causing it.

It's a victorious breakthrough in our beginning to understand depression. However, we must be careful not to downplay the struggle. Thoughts aren't easily changed. Especially those thoughts that developed in childhood that have now become beliefs. But this knowledge does create a road map for healing. If working on our thoughts and beliefs can help break us out of the depression, at least we have a place to start.

I love when the Word jumps off the page to speak to the reality of our existence. So when I sought God for some inspired truth for this chapter, I was floored when he brought Psalm 77 to my attention during a church service the same day. I knew as soon as I heard it that it was meant for this book. Look with me at verses 1-5:

> I cried out to God for help;
>> I cried out to God to hear me.
> When I was in distress, I sought the Lord;
>> at night I stretched out untiring hands,
>> and I would not be comforted.
> I remembered you, God, and I groaned;
>> I meditated, and my spirit grew faint.

You kept my eyes from closing;
I was too troubled to speak.
I thought about the former days, the years of long ago.

Crying out with tears. The picture of desperation from untiring hands. Distress and an inability to be comforted. Weariness and fatigue. Difficulty sleeping. Difficulty speaking. Getting stuck in the past. If this isn't a picture of depression, then I don't know what is. No one is sure who this psalmist is, but he's clearly going through it. The psalmist then does something that may be familiar to us. He puts his frustration, anger, fears, and feelings of forsakenness on God. In verses 6-9, he cries out:

My heart meditated and my spirit asked:
"Will the Lord reject forever?
Will he never show his favor again?
Has his unfailing love vanished forever?
Has his promise failed for all time?
Has God forgotten to be merciful?
Has he in anger withheld his compassion?"

More real feelings. More real words. It would be hard to judge him for this. Which one of us hasn't been in this place? Which one of us hasn't felt rejected or abandoned by God at times? The feelings aren't so far down that we don't feel them in trouble and heartache. And they're certainly not beyond a minute's reach in our pain and depression.

But right after these cries are the most powerful words in the whole passage, in my opinion. Words that reveal a timeless secret. Words that give power back into the psalmist's hands. Words that begin to heal his heart. Something shifts for the psalmist when in verse 10 he says, "Then I thought."

And then he thought. Y'all, sit with this a moment. And then he thought.

Just short of cursing God for forsaking him, he thought.

He thought to think about his pain a little differently.

He thought to remember the ways God had reached out and saved him before (v. 10).

He thought to meditate, to focus singly on God's might and power (v. 12).

He thought to worship God's holiness and the fact that his ways are not our ways (v. 13).

He thought to proclaim that God is a God of miracles (v. 14).

He thought to declare that God is a God of redemption (v. 15).

He thought to remember who he was calling out to in his distress. And these new thoughts transformed his inner world.

We can't be sure how long this transformation took. We don't know if it took days, weeks, months, or even years. But we can be sure of the fact that the psalmist focused on changing his thoughts. The wisdom of Scripture shines through here again. The wisdom of modern science is just catching up.

Reason #2: loneliness and disconnection. In 2018, Cigna conducted a large national poll to assess levels of loneliness and explore its impact in people's lives and in the workplace. They found that 54 percent of Americans reported feeling lonely. In 2019, they conducted the same survey and found that 61 percent of Americans now reported feeling lonely.[5] That's three in five Americans. Loneliness has been an epidemic in the United States for a while now and it's only on the rise.

Another notable finding is that loneliness is prevalent across generations. Gen Z—those between eighteen and twenty-two years old—reported the highest loneliness scores (50 out of 80 total points), as compared to boomers, who reported the lowest (43 out of 80 points), a level that still raised concern. Heavy social media use was also linked to loneliness, with 73 percent of very heavy social media users reporting loneliness compared to 52 percent of light users. This is an issue. This matters.

Loneliness has been consistently linked to both physical and mental health issues. In one study, loneliness expert John Cacioppo took 135 people who had been identified as highly lonely and brought them into his lab at the University of Chicago for a day.[6] In a first round of study, the group was instructed to complete personality tests. They showed higher levels of anxiety, lower self-esteem, and pessimism. This wasn't a surprise to Cacioppo, as loneliness studies had long linked loneliness to poorer well-being.

But he wanted to look specifically at the impact of loneliness on depression. So he split this group into two groups, group A and group B, and gave them different instructions. Group A was instructed to remember and reflect on periods in their lives when they were really lonely. Group B was instructed to remember the opposite—a time in their lives when they felt really connected. After a space of reflection, he had both groups take personality tests again.

What he found was significant: those who were instructed to feel lonely became radically more depressed, while those who were instructed to feel connected became radically less depressed. There was a crystal clear directional link here. Loneliness led to depression.

It's hardly an exaggeration to say loneliness kills, and certainly not an exaggeration to say loneliness hurts.

It's important to remember that loneliness isn't about being alone. Some people can have very few friends and be socially fulfilled, while others can have hundreds of friends and feel profoundly disconnected. Loneliness is more about the quality of the connection. It also appears that what matters most in our connections is a feeling of something shared. Loneliness is what happens when you're not sharing anything that matters to you with anyone else.

This could be the reason why some married couples feel so strongly connected while raising kids together but then become strangers once the last kid goes off to college. It could be the reason why shared heartbreak makes certain people fall in love, even when it's not a good fit, not the right time, or otherwise inappropriate. Sharing things that matter draws us together.

What matters to you, and who are you sharing it with? How deep are your current connections? If depression is knocking at your door, these are questions that must be answered. In fact, these are vital questions for us all.

Reason #3: loss of meaning. Sometimes life feels as though it's drained of its meaning. You're no longer sure why you're getting up every day. You have no idea what you're really doing at work. You begin to question what you're really living for or why you're here. Sometimes it's not the deep questions that trouble you but a profound sense of emptiness. You feel like something is missing. You're not sure what this something is, but you know it's vital. The emptiness in your soul tells you it is. You can't find answers. You feel lost. This is a hard place to be, but so many live there. It's a dark town with many neighbors, none who quite know how to help.

In a *New York Times* opinion piece, behavioral scientist Dr. Clay Routledge made a bold claim about the rise of suicide in the United States, which the CDC recently reported has gone up 25 percent since 1999. He claimed that our problem with suicide isn't an issue of access to mental health treatment. In fact, more people are seeking help than have before. Our problem is a "crisis of meaninglessness."[7] And it looks like his argument is worth considering. Loss of meaning in life has been linked consistently with substance abuse, anxiety, depression, and suicide. It's a big deal.

Social psychologist Roy F. Baumeister analyzed research across a wide range of disciplines and found that we seek meaning for our lives in four ways.

We need to feel like our current engagements and activities are related to and working toward a future outcome. This is a sense of purpose.

We need to feel like our actions reflect some sort of moral value— for example, value for justice, freedom, liberation, helping, healing, family, respect.

We need to feel effective. We need to feel that we have enough power and control over our outcomes to truly make a difference in some positive way.

We need to feel a positive sense of self-worth. Namely, we need to feel valuable to others and also distinctive from everyone else.

All four needs—purpose, moral value, self-efficacy, and positive self-worth—must play out in our daily lives for us to feel like our lives have meaning. But all four needs can be compromised by experiences like mundane work, social exclusion, and rejection. We need to feel that we are meaningfully a part of something bigger than ourselves.

SOME SIMPLER REASONS FOR DEPRESSION?

We've looked at the big stuff. The power of thought and its relationship to brain chemistry, the problem with loneliness, and the impact of the loss of meaning. They each give us a way to understand depression and its causes in a new, fresh way. But could there be some simpler stuff at work?

Professor and researcher Dr. Stephen Ilardi says yes. In his book *The Depression Cure,*[8] Dr. Ilardi outlines six factors that have been linked to lowering depressive symptoms and guarding the brain from depression in the first place. In addition to thought management and social connection, Ilardi argues that there are four simple lifestyle changes we can make to nurture our mental health. Based on his research findings, he suggests:

- *More omega-3 (and less sugar).* Dr. Ilardi shares that the lowest rates of depression are found in countries with the highest levels of omega-3 in their diets. (Think fish, nuts, seeds, and leafy veggies.) In contrast, diets high in sugar activate inflammatory responses in the brain and suppress the activity of an important hormone—brain-derived neurotrophic factor (BDNF)—that is important for happiness. People with depression have low levels of this hormone.

- *More physical activity.* Physical activity elevates levels of BDNF and activates serotonin, another important brain chemical that regulates mood and energy. Researchers at Duke also compared the impact of Zoloft, a popular antidepressant that targets serotonin, to the effect of exercise and found that just thirty minutes of brisk walking a day was as effective as using the medication.

- *More sunlight.* Sunlight activates the brain through receptors in the eye that receive the sensory information. Our brains love sunlight. In fact, a few other studies have found light therapy to be an effective treatment for depression in some individuals, operating in the brain similar to an antidepressant.

- *More sleep.* Dr. Ilardi shares research findings that show most episodes of depression follow several weeks of poor sleep. The implication here being that disrupted sleep isn't just a symptom of depression, it can lead to depression. For this reason, he recommends we get eight hours of quality sleep every night and make it a priority to overcome the obstacles that get in the way of that. If sleep has become a problem for you, it's time to start paying attention.

FOLLOW YOUR PAIN AND
UNCOVER YOUR THOUGHTS

In the show *All American*, the traumas of a young Black man from South Central Los Angeles are on full display as he pursues his dream of playing professional football. We, of course, get to follow his love interest, a girl named Layla, whose mother died in a car accident and whose father abandoned her in the aftermath, likely due to his own inability to cope. Layla lives in her big Beverly Hills mansion alone.

Over a few episodes, we follow her journey into depression and suicidality and ultimately into a treatment center where she's encouraged to reveal her broken truth: "I don't think the people in my life love me enough to stay," she says to a quieted room. It's a beautiful scene that sensitively and accurately portrays the reality of depression. Sometimes it's purely a product of our past pain.

There's no getting around the fact depression is often a cry for the deep wounds to be noticed. It's a cry from the abuse, the neglect, and the rejection. It's a cry from the sense of failure, the shame, and the loss. These cries must be answered. Relatedly, the thoughts that have formed must be excavated and examined. They must be held up to the light and exposed. This is for good reason. Dr. Caroline Leaf shared a nugget from her work in an interview with a pastor, saying, "The minute you're aware of something, it's weakened. Anything that's weakened is changeable."

I couldn't have said it better. The only way we can begin to work on our thoughts is to be able to talk about them. Pain freezes our thoughts in time, but conversation dislodges them. We need to be open to the process and commit to the work of bringing our worst thoughts into God's light and love.

If you sense that your depression is connected to some unresolved things of your past, begin a relationship with a licensed mental health professional. Deep trauma work requires assistance. Real thought work requires support. (I've got a chapter at the end solely devoted to this process, and I highly suggest you make use of it.) If for whatever reason you're still not ready, a good first step would be seeking quality trauma and thought-work resources. If this is the path you take, do enough research to ensure that the source of support will be legitimate. Make sure you're learning from those who are trained.

COME OUT OF YOUR LONELINESS

The three most important relationships in our lives are our relationships with God, others, and ourselves. The importance of our relationship with God is self-explanatory. The importance of our relationship with self is becoming more recognized, and I couldn't be happier to see our culture rally around ideas of self-care and self-love. But we can't ignore research that points to our need for meaningful connections with others. We are deeply in need of real community and friends. Quality people time matters.

If you're an introvert or self-proclaimed loner, please don't freak out. I'm certainly not telling you to be with people all day. I'm an introvert myself, and just the thought of that drains me. I enjoy being alone and can stay in a bedroom by myself for days. In fact, growing up, my family would call my room "the cave" because once I went in, I never came out. However, when I felt like connecting, there was someone to connect with. When I felt like sharing a piece of myself or my journey, there was someone to share that with too. It's a blessing that I want for you as well. A blessing we can choose.

I challenge you today to become more intentional. Make the choice to nurture the relationships you already have, or seek real opportunity to begin new ones. When appropriate, try sending a friend a message like this:

> *Hi . . . I really value our friendship. I don't know if I've shared this with you yet, but I've been struggling with sadness/depression. I'm not afraid of it, and I'm currently learning to understand it. But one thing I've learned is that I need meaningful connection. I'd like to be more intentional about connecting with the people I love and cherish and help me feel like I belong/help me feel at home. You come to mind as one of those people in my life. Are you up for connecting soon? Maybe we could _____. (List meaningful ways to share time like conversation over coffee, nature, a beach day, a day of pure enjoyment at Disneyland, etc.)*

I can't imagine a true friend would ever turn down such intention, vulnerability, hope, and resilience. I'm excited just thinking about the future dates with friends and loved ones you're about to have. Talk about healing!

FIND MEANING AGAIN

With the research on depression potentially pointing to a problem with meaninglessness, it's vital that we rediscover a sense of meaning for our lives.

Have you ever looked up the definition of *meaning*? I find it telling. According to Merriam-Webster, the word *meaning* refers to the thing that one intends to convey. I love this. I love that this definition helps clarify in a nutshell what we all hope for our lives: That our life will convey something. That our life will send an important message through how we do it, share it, and live it overall. That our lives will uplift, empower, heal, help, move, touch, bring light to another. In short, that our life matters. In some way, to somebody.

To bring in Baumeister's points, we convey this message when we are able to live out our sense of purpose, honor our moral values, feel effective in our lives, and be affirmed in our self-worth. Without these things, we create a breeding ground for void, emptiness, and depression. This isn't of God. He created us to experience more.

So how do we rediscover meaning? How do live out our message or get back in touch with it when we begin to lose sight? Well, meaning has always required that we connect with something outside of ourselves. We cultivate meaning when we do things like help people, help an important cause, or do purposeful work.

Think about your days. Are they spent doing any one of these things?

Of course, life doesn't always make this easy. For one, these actions require energy, which may feel hard to come by when depression has you in its grip. To this I say, one tiny action—be it lending an ear, offering help, providing company—can go a long way. In fact, a 2017 study looked at the impacts of compassion goals (striving to help others, avoiding selfishness) versus self-image goals (obtaining approval from others, getting others to notice your positive values) on anxiety and depression.[9] Researchers found that participants reported greater depressive symptoms on days they were focused on

more self-image goals and fewer symptoms on days they were focused on more compassion goals. Turning one's attention to others
appeared to relieve daily experiences of depression to a degree. I love
that God has designed us in such a way that helping to heal others
also helps heal ourselves.

When it comes to engaging in meaningful work, you may not have
the luxury of working an inherently fulfilling job. Your priority may be
putting food on the table and keeping a roof over your family's head
however you can. For this, you deserve utmost respect. But when
meaning isn't found naturally, you can create it for yourself.

Sometimes, with a perspective shift, you can do this right at your
job. Maybe there is a relationship you can build or a new project you
can start with a coworker. Otherwise, you can take small steps toward
new entrepreneurial ventures, creative endeavors, or plans to explore
more of life and God by traveling the world. No matter the case, there
is always something you can do to create more meaning in your life.
And your joy and freedom from depression may depend on it.

WILL YOU CHOOSE LIFE?

No matter the cause, fighting depression is hard. There is no quick fix,
overnight potion, or miracle cure. But there is the power that God has
given you to overcome. Power that begins with a choice.

Deuteronomy 30:19 says: "This day I call the heavens and the earth
as witnesses against you that I have set before you life and death,
blessings and curses. Now choose life, so that you and your children
may live."

God has given us free will and the power to choose in our lives.
And we can assume this power doesn't just apply to our spiritual
lives but also to our physical, mental, and emotional lives. They all
work together. That's how God created us. We can reflect and debate
on what "life" versus "death" looks like in these areas, but health,
wealth, and wholeness come to mind as I consider the wisdom of

both life and Scripture. We have the ability to choose what we want, accept, and pursue in our lives. We have the power to choose what we'll fight for.

Remember Joy's story from the top of this chapter. The power of choice was a turning point in her life. Though her healing journey had just begun, her path was clear. She would fight depression. She would not accept it as her end. She writes:

> Easter that year was significant for me. I don't remember the exact message, but I do remember leaving church thinking that if Jesus resurrected, I could too. That day became the day I decided I had to fight. My name was Joy, and I wasn't going to go out like that. I was going to beat this. I was going to rise.

So what will it be? What will we chase? Will it be life? It seems God is leaving much up to us.

ENVY

Our Need for Enoughness

Nothing sharpens sight like envy.

THOMAS FULLER

Envy is thin because it bites but never eats.

SPANISH PROVERB

People hate those who make them feel their own inferiority.

LORD CHESTERFIELD

*Beggars do not envy millionaires, though of course they
will envy other beggars who are more successful.*

BERTRAND RUSSELL

ANDREA'S STORY
I RESENTED HER

*I resented her. I'm embarrassed to admit it but I did. I didn't know her
personally, but I'd followed her on social media long enough to know
details of her journey. She was young, she was just starting medical*

residency, and she had dreams of working as a professional in the media. We had similar goals. She was transparent about this and called on her followers often to help her achieve goals she hoped would get her noticed. Her calls to action worked. Daily, I watched her following grow by thousands as she pumped out perfectly crafted tweets about health and self-care. She also put out all kinds of digital products I swear she whipped up overnight. She was starting to get those features in the media.

I was amused by it all at first. She was a self-marketing genius, but a lot of her content was misleading, pseudoscience stuff or just plain wrong. She clearly needed to finish her training. Then I got angry. Here I was fully into my career, research to my name, and almost ten years of trying to make a name for myself. Still, I hadn't garnered half of the support and excitement she had, and she'd only been doing this a couple years. Her success seemed effortless, and mine seemed perpetually stunted. When I finally opened up about it at a personal development workshop, things became clear. It wasn't so much her social media success I wanted; it was her freedom. This girl had all the confidence in the world. She didn't care how young she was, she didn't care about what she didn't know, and she didn't care about what others thought of her goals and platform. She was living her best life, however imperfectly, and she was thriving.

Meanwhile, though I had much to offer, I was stuck. I struggled with imposter syndrome. I obsessed about making things perfect, which slowed me down significantly. I feared criticism more than anything else. I had tons of ideas, but they never felt good enough to execute. Somewhere deep down I believed I was bound to fail.

HIDING ENVY

I've had enough conversations in my work and personal life to know that envy can be difficult to acknowledge. It's uncomfortable to admit. The feeling of envy often stirs up shame and embarrassment because for many, envy feels really ugly.

Perhaps this is because envy is one of the only emotions we experience that has been put squarely in the sin category. The Word doesn't seem to take the issue lightly. We've got proverbs telling us that envy will rot our bones (Proverbs 14:30). We've got New Testament letters telling us to rid ourselves of it (1 Peter 2:1). We've even got a whole commandment dedicated to it: "You shall not covet" (Exodus 20:17).

Envy is what motivated Cain to kill his brother Abel (Genesis 4). Envy is what turned King Saul against David (1 Samuel 18). Envy is what caused Joseph's brothers to conspire to kill him (Genesis 37). Envy is what caused a bunch of sinners to hand over Jesus to be killed (Mark 15:10).

But however ugly envy may appear to be, it's clear that it's a common human experience. There wouldn't be this much attention on it if it wasn't. Furthermore, just because we know something is "bad" for us and want to avoid it doesn't mean we won't struggle with it at times. Since our struggles don't go away when we ignore them, envy, like any other emotion, is worth looking at. The more we understand what it means and what it reveals in our lives, the better we can deal with it.

THESE ARE A FEW OF THOSE ENVIABLE THINGS

A 2015 study surveyed over nine hundred adults about their struggle with envy.[1] In the study, over 75 percent of the volunteers admitted to experiencing envy over the past year. Among these people, envy was experienced in both close and distant relationships, but it was targeted mostly at people of the same gender and of similar age as the volunteers.

Moreover, what people were envious about shifted over the lifespan. Physical appearance and success academically, socially, and romantically were more enviable in early adulthood but lessened with age. Money, however, was more envied with age. Luckiness and a sense that someone has an overall better life stayed fairly consistent across the lifespan.

How might you have responded had you taken the survey? Would looks, money, or success have been on your list? Would it be someone's reputation, personality, or career? What about someone's love life, marriage, or family? What about someone's talent? Influence? Or something as pure as happiness? The point is, if we are honest with ourselves, we've probably felt envy at one point or another, and probably within the last year. But envy shouldn't make us feel bad about ourselves. It should make us curious.

THE ANATOMY OF ENVY

Aristotle once defined envy as "pain at the sight of another's good fortune" caused by "those who have what we ought to have."[2] It's a brutally honest way of looking at it, but it works. Additionally, envy has three components.

Awareness. You can't be envious of what someone has if you're not first aware that they have it. Pretty intuitive right? With envy, you are aware of the advantages or opportunities awarded someone else. You can see it, you can smell it, you can taste it, and you can imagine what it's like. This is part of what makes social media, and especially visual platforms like Instagram, a prime place to develop envy. Social media will make you aware of every single advantage and opportunity somebody has, whether you want to be aware or not.

Desire. Envy also requires desire. You can be aware of the advantages and opportunities awarded to someone but not feel envy because you don't necessarily desire these things for yourself. However, desire can be birthed later in our lives. New seasons and situations can fan its flames. Desire can also develop from the people around us. Sometimes we want something simply because of what it looks like on someone else.

I remember an interview where someone asked me about my top goals. I shared a few and then threw in "traveling the world." It sounded right, but as soon as I said it I knew it wasn't totally mine. Y'all, I hate flying. I talk myself down from anxiety attacks half the time. I despise when strangers talk to me midflight because I know that once that plane starts bumping, I'm going to have to throw my head in my knees, which awkwardly shuts the whole conversation down. The answer I gave didn't come from me. It came from recent scrolls down my timeline featuring perfectly curated photos of my beautiful friends in Tulum, Morocco, and Dubai. Before that interview, I was perfectly content with two-hour travels by car from Los Angeles to San Diego. I'm working through this phobia, but let me not lie to you all. At this very moment, I'm still quite content!

Anger and resentment. The last component of envy is anger. Some may even feel resentment or hostility. You don't just desire the unique advantages and opportunities awarded a person; you're a bit bothered they have it.

Maybe it feels unwarranted. Maybe thoughts like, *What did they do to deserve this?* swarm around in your head, and you can't deny the sinking feeling that life is just easier for some. Some people are just lucky. Some people have the right family, friends, and connections. You, on the other hand, didn't come into the world with any of these things. Then again, no one ever said life was fair.

Or maybe it feels unjust. You're a hard-working person, and you've been doing your part. You've been faithful. You've been patient. You've been generous. You've honored God with your heart and soul, and you've put in those prayers. Your obedience was supposed to guarantee the blessings, but you look up and those blessings seemed to have landed everywhere else. It's frustrating, maddening even, and it can be downright debilitating. No one wants to feel envy, but in the way we sometimes experience these moments, the anger of envy makes sense.

NOT ALL ENVY IS CREATED EQUAL

However, not all envy is created equal. Envy is a highly nuanced emotion, but its nuances have been eclipsed by the limitations of language. The English language uses one word to describe the feeling of envy. Envy is envy and it's all bad. Other languages—including Dutch, Polish, German, and Thai—have two different words for envy, implying there are two types.[3] Let's look at how researchers have distinguished at least two types of envy—malicious envy and benign envy. It's fascinating.

Malicious envy. Malicious envy is the kind of envy that probably first comes to mind when you think of the sin of envy. It's the kind of envy that motivates you to destroy. Malicious envy is not what we want festering in our hearts. However, even malicious envy has its motivations.

Consider this scenario. You give someone your best efforts and they turn around, point menacingly at you, and accuse you of being useless and inept. They tell you you've wasted their time. How angry, resentful, and disillusioned might you feel? Probably very.

Well, this is what's happening in the case of malicious envy. Except the critical inner voice in your own head is doing the accusing. You're the one telling yourself you're inferior. You're the one calling yourself inept. But since this was triggered by something you saw in someone else, you turn on them. You get angry at the person who shed light on your inadequacies. From this point on, your goal may be to make them shine a little less. So you start spreading a little gossip. Or you try and get others to see them in a negative light too. Or you just pull back and stop engaging with them, even if you once considered them a friend. If they continue to shine, at least it won't be through your window.

Benign envy. *Benign envy* is the term used to describe the feeling of awareness and desire of someone's life that causes you to want to match them. It's still an uncomfortable feeling, but it drives you to action. Benign envy spurs curiosity. What gifts, talents, and skills do I share with this person I "envy" that I can begin to put to good use? What can I leverage in my own life that can lessen the gap between where I am and where I want to be? Who in my network can I reach out to? Everybody gets a little help, right? Benign envy drives strategy. Between an honest examination of one's skills and resources and some strategy to capitalize on it all, benign envy can actually help motivate us to operate at our best. If you're a native English speaker, this may be an uncomfortable idea to embrace. But consider that your discomfort is because we've only been taught one way.

CONDITIONS FOR ENVY

You probably don't envy everyone. In fact, you probably don't envy most people. There are many more people in your life who you genuinely celebrate and many more who you love to see win. This is beautiful and healthy and important. Which one of us doesn't have "rejoices when I rejoice" on our list of prerequisites for people we dare to call friends? We support people we love and expect they do the same for us. Envy isn't an issue in most of our relationships.

Researchers of envy, such as Richard Smith and his team from the University of Kentucky, have identified what makes it easier to envy some and not others.[4] They found the following.

The object of your envy must be relevant to you. The object of your envy must have or be able to do something that you find personally meaningful. I think gymnastics is the most incredible sport in the world. I think Simone Biles is one of the most incredible athletes in the world. Have you seen that girl move? Have you seen what happens after she moves? She is instantly and virally celebrated; clips of her in action are shared by people in Hollywood, other athletes, and practically everyone else. I'm right there with them. I've also never wanted to be a competitive gymnast. Couldn't be one if I tried. Simone can collect all the gold medals and break all the records, and I'll continue to cheer her on. You probably will too.

Greatness is inspiring and very easy to celebrate. Even easier when it's happening in a lane you never saw yourself in.

The object of your envy must be similar or comparable to you. A person could possess what you dream of and what you desperately want, but if they are in some way incomparable to you, you likely won't be envious of them.

I've been known to say I want to be like Oprah. I dream of being able to do what she's done with her influence. I dream of having my hands in as many creative projects as she does. I dream of the wealth and the legacy she's built as a Black woman, especially one from humble beginnings. But I've never envied Oprah. Oprah is light years ahead of me. Oprah started her journey decades before me. Oprah is currently a billionaire, and my bank account is far more humbling. As my dad would say in his Nigerian way: "Oprah is not our mate." Touché, Pops. Touché.

We won't feel envy toward the Oprahs in our lives. We'll feel it toward the people with a similar start line, in a similar race. People who look like us and act like us. People our same age. People who graduated when we graduated or started their business the year we did. Because when people similar to us have something we don't, our perceived lack of progress feels personal. It's much harder to explain. The gap between where they are and where we are seems to point to a problem within ourselves. And that's the real problem of envy.

OUR NEED FOR ENOUGHNESS

"What's making you put so much pressure on yourself?"

It was a question my therapist had asked me during one of our sessions, and I honestly didn't have an answer. I had just shared with her that the night before I had caught myself feeling like I wasn't doing enough with my life. It was clearly triggered by an update from a friend who had shared another notch of her success. I'd been rooting for her for years and should have been happy, but instead I found myself negatively focused inward. This was someone from my same background and my same age, and she'd been scratching off her goals left and right that year. All I could think was that I wasn't doing enough and that I was falling behind.

My therapist challenged my thinking. She pointed out the many accomplishments I too had under my belt. Things I thought would come much later in my life but were now very much behind me. I felt her looking at me with eyes that said, *Girl, what's not enough about all that?* But I just looked right back at her. I still didn't have an answer.

Then she came right out with it: "It's like . . . It's like you're trying to prove your worth."

And there it was. The tears welled as I admitted to her that there was something to that. It wasn't something I saw until that moment, and it wasn't something I'd felt in years. I admitted I was a little embarrassed by the feeling, which she quickly shut down. She reminded me of the ways so many of us try to prove our worth. We do it in different times and seasons, and there are so many different ways it manifests. Pangs of envy are just one of them. I thought about my spaces of influence and even a few of my recent conversations and knew she was right. If there is one thing that unifies us as humans, it's our resistance to believing we're enough.

Envy is a problem with our sense of worthiness. And we won't feel worthy of anything unless we feel like we're enough. When I teach about enoughness, I start with a basic definition. Look at how Merriam-Webster defines the word *enough*: "occurring in such quantity, quality, or scope as to fully meet demands, needs, or expectations."

I love it every time I read it. When we believe that we are enough, we believe that within ourselves we have as much quantity, quality, and scope of whatever is needed to fully meet the demands and expectations of our lives.

Whatever is required of relationships—the ones we have and the ones we desire—we have enough of it.

Whatever is required of our career, we have enough of it.

Whatever is required of success, we have enough of it.

Whatever is required of lasting impact and influence, we have enough of it.

Whatever is required for joy and happiness, we have enough of it.

Whatever is required for the dreams of our hearts, we have enough of it.

Whatever is required of the calling God put on our lives, we have enough of it.

For everything God has created, designed, and planned for our lives, we are enough for it. We don't need anything more than what we already have.

This is why enoughness doesn't need approval or external validation. These things are nice and encouraging, but they are simply a confirmation of what is believed already about the self.

Enoughness certainly doesn't need to prove itself either. People walking in enoughness do things because they want to. Because they truly love to. Because it brings them happiness, joy, and peace. They could do it for thousands of people if needed, but they could also happily do it just for themselves. It doesn't matter who is or isn't watching. That's the stamp of enoughness. It's freedom from all the things the world says one has to do and be to be worthy. Enoughness gives us our sense of worth.

Telling ourselves we're enough should be a daily practice. We need to reflect our enoughness back to ourselves. This may require that you speak to the part of you that needs this most. The little girl or little boy inside you who didn't hear it enough. The seven-, eleven-, or sixteen-year-old inside you who experienced something that made this difficult to take in. You need to speak to yourself like you would speak to them. Hold their image in your mind as you tell yourself:

- You are worthy.
- You are enough.

- There is nothing more you need to do for my love and attention.

- There's absolutely nothing you need to prove.

- You are wonderful as you are.

Sometimes envy is just the pain of believing we are not enough. Everything changes once we remember that we are.

WHAT ARE YOU *REALLY* MISSING?

As we tend to our need for enoughness, we'll need to acknowledge another reality. Envy sometimes points to a deeper need. In Andrea's story from the top of the chapter, her envy seemed initially to be about social media success, but it was really about her desire to be free from her fears. What are your true desires? It's an important question.

Admittedly, one of my favorite shows of all time is *Gossip Girl*. It centers around a pair of filthy rich best friends—Serena van der Woodsen and Blair Waldorf—who try to navigate their Upper East Side, New York, lives amid young love, family legacy, and the challenges of growing up. A running theme in the show is Blair's envy for Serena— the dazzling blond whose success always seems effortless. In one iconic scene, Blair has to follow Serena's college entrance interview to Yale, and the dean point-blank asks her to share something that's not in her folder. Caught off guard, she admits with haunting vulnerability:

> Well, I'm aware I lack some people's easy grace with strangers, and I don't exactly make you feel like you've known me forever even though we just met. When I laugh you might not smile just at the coquettish sound of it . . . and my hair might not sparkle when it catches the light. [But] everything worth knowing about me is in that envelope. I made sure of it.

The scene ends and you're left empathizing with Blair. This was obviously not about goodness with strangers, laughter, or sparkling hair. This was about that sinking feeling that you're not quite what everybody else seems to want. We've likely all resonated with Blair at some point in our lives, and we've likely all needed what she needed then: an honest, meaningful reminder that she was enough, exactly as she was. And more so, she was good enough to be *accepted*.

Recall our discussion on the deep needs of our being—needs for safety, belonging, significance, growth, and contribution. Envy is hardly ever about the little things. This is why some can accumulate the wealth of the world and still not be happy. Or why some can become a sensation, be celebrated around the world, and still feel like something's missing. It's never really about the external things. It's always about the deep needs. What are yours?

THE THING ABOUT COMPARISON

You've heard them all before: *Don't compare yourself to others. Comparison is the thief of joy. Comparison kills.* There are tons of redirectives out there for comparison, and with good reason. Comparison is a prerequisite for envy. Comparison can quite literally make us sick. That's because if we are not careful, comparison can rob us of the joy of our own journey. It can steal the thunder from our own wins.

Have you ever been excited about an opportunity or win, only to get an update from a friend, in real life or social media, and all of a sudden feel like your win isn't a big deal? That is the robbery of comparison. The excitement, pride, and satisfaction you appropriately felt for yourself suddenly disappear, and you're back to feeling like you don't measure up. This kind of lock-and-step comparison is a dangerous trap. It disrespects all of the hard work you've put in to get to where you are. It dishonors the beauty and diversity of your unique journey. It's a rejection of the different things working together for your ultimate good, and it's something we need to firmly tell ourselves to stop.

But as we begin to meet the real needs of envy, comparison can take on new meaning. As in the case of benign envy, comparison doesn't have to be all bad. When used judiciously, comparison can be useful for our growth.

There will be times we feel stuck in our lives. Times where we want to be healthier, happier, fitter, freer, and more successful in our lives and relationships. Times where we need a good dose of inspiration and motivation. Times where we need a kick in the pants. Well, guess where all this comes from? You already know. Other people.

Comparison can show what's possible for us. Especially when the object of our comparison is similar to us, which it usually is. The success stories of people with similar traits, skills, and backgrounds can give us a sense of what's also in our reach. We can be inspired and motivated if we can make some mental shifts. For example, a shift from competition to celebration would be important. It may look like moving from "I'm in competition with you" to "Wow, thank you for showing me what's possible for me!"

But another, perhaps more important, shift might be moving from a sense of scarcity to a belief in abundance. This may look like moving from "You have taken what I want and there is no more left for me" to "There's a great big abundant world out there, and I will find joy in figuring out what's out there waiting for me."

Note that a scarcity mindset usually starts in childhood and may fester in your life as a problematic core belief. If believing in abundance is difficult for you, this would be a great thing to unpack. At the end of the day, a feeling of enoughness is what fuels the idea that you are cut out for the task of figuring out your journey and worthy enough to receive good things.

However, *to create a growth opportunity out of comparison and envy, you must take action.* Sitting back and watching other people reach their goals won't be helpful or productive. Healthy, productive comparison leads to healthy, productive moves. So maybe you need an action plan and a new strategy. Maybe you need an updated vision. Or maybe you just need to reach out to the person you've been watching awhile and ask for advice. This could be a great way to cut through the negative noise in your head. If you can connect, tell them what you admire about them. Tell them how you've been inspired. Then practice humility and vulnerability. Share your trouble spots and see if they are willing to share something that might help.

SOCIAL MEDIA: FANNING FLAMES OF ENVY

We also have to acknowledge that nothing fans the flames of unhealthy comparison and envy more than social media. Social media amplifies whatever internal psychological conflicts we already have. It gives our insecurities a field day.

For one, the nature of social media makes it impossible for the brain to catch a break (needed for healthy comparison). Even if you wanted to pull back and rethink the messages you are sending yourself while you're on social media, it's impossible. Not until you log off and take a break. These platforms constantly bombard us with messages and information. Some updates may be necessary but most are not.

Clinical psychologist Rachel Andrew said it best when she noted that social media has made "everyone accessible for comparison. In the past people might have just envied their neighbors, but now we can compare ourselves with everyone across the world."[5]

We don't need this. We don't need to know how much is in Jon's bank account. We don't need to see every glamorous trip Sarah took. We don't need weekly updates about every amazing thing that happened in Paul's or Lilian's life. It was exciting at first, but now it's just brain overload. The brain does well with things that it needs. It doesn't do well with floods.

Additionally, social media exploits us. In the field of computer science, the word *exploit* is defined as a software tool designed to take advantage of a flaw in a computer system, typically for malicious intent. We are not computers, but this is exactly what social media

does to our psychological system. It takes advantage of our fundamental needs to be liked, validated, seen, and included and preys on
them. It takes advantage of our human vulnerabilities for its own
gain. That gain, of course, is money.

Part of the way social networks make money is through investors
and advertisers needing us to spend time on their platforms. But for
this to work, they must keep their users obsessively engaged. Our
need for likes, validation, approval, status, and popularity is the
perfect ingredient. People make their money and everyone's happy.
Everyone except the social media users, of course, who are more
anxious, insecure, and depressed than they've ever been. Until there's
a way to use social media without being exploited by it, the psychological ramifications may outweigh the benefits. At the very least,
when we log on to our social media apps, we should do so con-
sciously and with care.

GOD CHOSE THE WEAK THINGS OF THE WORLD

One of my life inspirations is a seven-figure-making speaker, author,
and business coach. But despite being positioned in the business
world, she is also boldly unapologetic about her faith. There's always
been much to celebrate about her, to be honest, and perhaps even
more so now. Because in the middle of all her successes, she is a
woman in her early forties who just gave birth to . . . triplets!

I can't say I know her full story. I don't know how difficult her
journey to motherhood has been. But I do know what the world says
about the right time for entering motherhood. I'm familiar with the
less than favorable narratives that exist about ambitious, career-
driven women. I've been fed these messages myself. And I do know
the statistics stacked against Black women, in particular, in the areas
of marriage and family.

So when my mentor dropped the news that she and her doting
husband were pregnant with not one, not two, but three babies, I

joined so many women in happy tears. This was a win for all of us alike. "It's a blessing to walk in your miracle," she later said, "especially after praying and walking with others in theirs." Whew. What a testimony.

Her story brought me back to 1 Corinthians 1:27-29, which says:

> But God chose the foolish things of the world to shame the wise; God chose the weak things of the world to shame the strong. God chose the lowly things of this world and the despised things—and the things that are not—to nullify the things that are, so that no one may boast before him.

I wonder how much we groan about things in our lives that God actually has a bigger plan for. I wonder how much we despise the perceived lack in our lives for which God has intention. What if God wanted to defy statistics and break stereotypes through our lives and adversities? What if right now there are things in transit in our lives that will be a testament to God's glory? It's a beautiful thing to finally have what you want. But it can be an even more beautiful thing when you don't have it yet. Especially when God's sovereign above it all. Which he is.

LOOKING INWARD

The focus of your envy is outside of you, but the problem stems from within. So when you feel the pain of envy rising up, it's time to look inward. Inward without judging or condemning yourself for it. Inward without hating yourself for it. Inward with the full intention of allowing God to shine his light. Because without paying attention and dealing with your envy head on, you open the door to behaving badly. And that's not okay either. You don't get permission here to gossip, pull people down, or find some way to frustrate their efforts. My friends call this being an enemy of progress. You don't want to be one of those. Really the only person you'll end up blocking is yourself.

When you're ready to get to work, create a quiet space and have a journal ready. Reflect on these questions and write your answers down. Bring to mind a current, recent, or memorable case of envy in your life. Ask yourself

- *What's the context?*
  - ▶ What was the envy about? What did you see or hear? What was said, how was it said, and who said it?
  - ▶ If the object of envy is an inanimate object or experience (e.g., a product, travel experience), ask yourself what these things symbolize. Is it wealth? Security? Freedom? Affection?
  - ▶ If the object of envy is a person, do the same, but separate the person from the object. What does this person possess, and what does it mean to you? Beauty? Status? Opportunity? Satisfaction?
  - ▶ What's the real need here? What are you really missing?
- *What's the story?*
  - ▶ What can't you have and why can't you have it? Is it because (currently in your mind) you're not pretty enough, smart enough, strong enough, popular enough, slim enough, brave enough? Something else? Are you too much of something? Do you have too little?
  - ▶ What narrative about yourself have you been feeding? What's the running commentary?
- *Where did this story come from?*
  - ▶ Who told you that you can't have it? Where is that coming from? What's the story's origin? When did the story begin?
  - ▶ How long have you been telling yourself this? Could this explain how deeply you believe in it?
- *What's the alternative? How can you challenge the narrative?*
  - ▶ Is there a real concern about your future? Should there be?

- ▶ Is there real concern about your capability? Should there be?

- ▶ Is there something you're trying to prove to yourself? If so, where is that coming from?

- ▶ Is there a belief, mindset, or worldview you hold that you might need to work out with a therapist?

- ▶ What would your life look like if you took away all the pressure to be anything but who you are right now? Can you allow yourself to be this person? Can you take the pressure off? Can you trust that doing something for love is enough?

- ▶ As things become more right within you, can you believe in yourself enough to get it done?

Recall that in Andrea's story, she envied another woman who seemed more confident in herself. When Andrea explored this in therapy, she made progress by answering some of these same questions herself.

When I brought this up with my therapist, he helped me see everything in a new way. I wasn't a bad person, but my feelings were misdirected. I wasn't angry with this other woman; I was frustrated with myself. I didn't trust that I could put myself out there and not be swallowed whole. I didn't trust that I had what anybody wanted. My goal was to figure out where this all came from.

I soon realized that I'd never felt truly accepted. I always felt like the odd one out and never felt like I truly belonged anywhere. This made it hard to take the risks I needed to take to be where I wanted to be. But as I learned more about my need for acceptance, I learned how to accept myself. I learned how to validate my own place and space in this world because needing others to do it was squeezing the life out of me. I needed my life back! I started to do things simply because I loved to do them and they made me happy. I did things that made me feel proud of my own self. I even got off social media for six months to remind myself what it's like to do life without the approval of an audience. It was the most freeing six months of my life. I clearly didn't need anyone else's life. All I needed was to approve and celebrate my own.

LOVE IS BLINDING

The phrase *love is blind* is usually taken to mean that when we are in love with someone, we don't see their faults. That works, but I see an alternative meaning. When we're totally in love, we don't see anyone else. The "perfect" person could walk past us on the beach, rock-hard abs and all, but it wouldn't matter; we wouldn't notice. The love we've got for the one we have is satisfying and complete. Squishy belly and everything. Love is not only blind, love is *blinding*. There is nothing else to see out there.

So it is with your own journey.

There's some incredible wisdom found in Galatians 6:4, which says, "Each one should test their own actions. Then they can take pride in themselves alone, without comparing themselves to someone else." I especially love how the NLT version puts it: "Pay careful attention to your own work, for then you will get the satisfaction of a job well done, and you won't need to compare yourself to anyone else."

Perhaps we cure envy with more love for ourselves. Perhaps we cure it with more respect for our journey. We may not have what we want, but we love what we've got. We may not be where we want to be, but we see where we're going and appreciate the steps we've already taken.

Who has gone through what you've gone through? Who has lost what you've lost, beaten what you've beaten, or defeated your demons? Whether the enemy likes it or not, you're still here. Your brilliance, resilience, strength, faith, and persistence warrant much celebration, if you can only see it. So put the blinders on, block out the noise, and look in the mirror. You're a champion.

SHAME

Our Need for Radical Love

Shame is the lie someone told you about yourself.

ANAIS NIN (ATTRIBUTED)

It's not always depression. Sometimes it's shame.

HILARY JACOBS HENDEL

*If we can share our story with someone who responds with
empathy and understanding, shame can't survive.*

BRENÉ BROWN

*One small crack does not mean that you are broken, it means
that you were put to the test and you didn't fall apart.*

LINDA POINDEXTER

*Toxic shame gives you a sense of worthlessness, a sense
of failing and falling short as a human being. Toxic
shame is a rupture of the self with the self.*

JOHN BRADSHAW

SHAVONNE'S STORY
I WAS BORN TO PARENTS ADDICTED TO DRUGS

I was born to parents addicted to drugs—can't think of anything more shameful than that. What kind of mother puts a needle in her arm while a baby grows in her belly? The answer would be mine. Mine did. Though she would eventually turn her life around, it was too little, too late. Fast living finally caught up with her, and when I was just ten, cancer took her life. My dad never did shake his habit, dying of kidney failure when I was sixteen. All my friends had parents to love them growing up but not me. I was desperate to know love. So I turned to where I thought I could get it and gave up the only thing I knew how to: my body.

Had I only known then what I know now: that no boy could fill the hole in my heart. No boy could fix the hurt in my spirit or heal the void my parents left me. But I got pregnant at nineteen, by a boy who didn't want a family and didn't want me. All I could ask was, Why? Why the addiction? Why all the death? Why the neglect? Why the abandonment? Why was this my story? Why, God? What was it about me? My shame was relentless.

AMY'S STORY
LOVE AT FIRST SIGHT GAVE ME AN STD

I just sat there and cried with my gynecologist. Thankfully she had some sort of emotional support training or something because she didn't kick me out. She told me I would be okay and tried to comfort me, but I couldn't be comforted. I had always been the responsible one. I was a good Christian girl who just . . . slipped up. This was supposed to be a routine checkup. How was this happening to me? I couldn't fathom telling anybody about this, so I let it all out with her. I told her how I thought I'd met my soulmate that year. How he spoke words of life into me. How I'd never felt so beautiful. I told her how he showered me with gifts and how he couldn't go a day without talking with me. I had prayed at the beginning of the year to meet my husband, and it seemed like I finally had. I fell hard and fast.

Then about a couple of months into our relationship, things drastically changed. His calls began to slow down. His sweet words diminished. It felt like I was frustrating him more and more by just being myself. I practiced abstinence, but I felt pressure to "keep" him. So, already feeling unlovable, I used sex as my last ditch effort to make him love me again. It didn't work. Soon I got a text that he was done with the relationship, and despite me blowing up his phone, I never heard from him again. I cried every day for months. I was angry with him, but even angrier with myself. Clearly, I wasn't good enough for him. I felt disappointed in myself.

Time passed and I began to recover. Then my calendar reminded me about my upcoming routine doctor's appointment, so I went. Nothing could have prepared for me the news about my tests. I was blindsided. I had an STD and needed to start treatment. He was the only one I had been with since renewing my commitment to Christ and abstinence. He gave me this. To say I felt shame was an understatement. What wasn't there to be ashamed about in my life?

THE MESSAGE OF SHAME

Shame has one goal in your life, and that's to make you feel that something is fundamentally wrong with you. It wants to make you feel deficient. It wants to make you feel defective. It wants to make you feel like you are damaged goods. And it will walk through many different doors to do so.

Shame enters our lives through trauma. The abuse, the neglect, the emotional abuse, and the bullying. Shame enters our lives through our hurt, discouragement, anxiety, depression, and the other difficult emotions we've worked through in this book. Shame enters our lives through circumstance also: Unemployment. Marriage failure. Losing your livelihood. Kids who aren't turning out like you raised them to be. Heartbreak. Perpetual singleness. STIs and STDs. Betrayal. Losing.

Failing. Falling. Underperforming. Being compared to someone else. Coming up short.

Shame rides into our lives on the wings of our insecurity and disappointment and whispers in our ears: *Something must be wrong with you. Why else would this be happening? This is your doing. This is your fault.* Shame is aggressive and subtle and strategic.

The pain of shame. The pain of shame is about belonging. As we know, God created us with this need to belong. Belonging is what turns us toward each other and toward him. It's the driving force of every relationship. We have a healthy dependence on each other because of it. In fact, belonging is such an integral part of our existence that our lives can be looked at as a collection of experiences singly focused on protecting it. Belonging is what gives our lives meaning and makes them rich and satisfying.

And shame knows this.

That's why the messages that shame sends—messages about our fundamental wrongness—are aimed at making us feel unworthy of belonging. When we are too wrong to belong, we are too wrong for love, affection, and connection. The logic of shame goes like this:

I am defective.

Defective people are unworthy of belonging (and therefore love, affection, and connection).

Therefore, I am unworthy of belonging (and love, affection, and connection).

Keep in mind that shame is hardly ever this conscious. We are not typically walking around thinking about how defective we are and how unworthy of belonging we must be. We won't even realize we feel and believe these things until sharp pains and big feelings suddenly come "out of nowhere."

Shame undercover. *I don't struggle with shame.* It's something you might have told yourself. However, part of the reason shame is so powerful is because it's so sophisticated in its presentation. It works undercover. Being able to heal from shame requires that we first be able to identify it when it shows up. So it's time to get hip to the game. Here are six silent ways shame operates in our lives:

1. *We hide.* I worked with a client once who felt so much unnecessary shame about gaining weight that she ejected herself from her own social life. She stopped going out, meeting up with friends, and even visiting her parents. Clearly her weight gain was attached to something deeper and created an intense fear of judgment and ridicule. She hid out to protect herself from what she believed would be unbearable to her.

   We won't all hide out in our homes though. We'll hide in our businesses and in busywork. We'll hide in our computers and phones. We'll hide in Netflix, Hulu, Amazon, Apple TV, Disney+, or whatever new streaming platform they'll come up with next. We'll hide in our social media profiles and filtered pictures. We'll hide in humor. We'll hide in alcohol and drugs. If it can separate us from a sense of smallness, we'll make it a home. The obvious problem here is that these things can't cover us up forever. At some point, we'll be forced to face ourselves.

2. *We blame.* I once worked with a young man who was going through a tough breakup. He reached out because he was "losing it" over the woman who had broken his heart. He just couldn't understand what went wrong. As we talked more, he kept coming back to her saying that he never took any responsibility for any wrongdoing and he never apologized for anything. I asked if there was any truth to it, and for a second he got quiet. Then the moment passed and he angrily ran down a list of her faults and all the reasons she was wrong for him. Perhaps there was some truth to what she said. Perhaps the real problem was his shame.

In a 2018 study, researchers found a link between apologizing and shame. After purposefully deceiving their college participants into thinking they were late to the research study, researchers observed their apologizing behaviors and analyzed what the students had previously reported about shame and guilt. The researchers found that the ease of apologizing was positively linked with guilt (that is, more guilt, more apologizing) but negatively linked to shame (meaning more shame, less apologizing), suggesting that there may be something about a true experience of shame that makes it difficult to say "I'm sorry." We will look at the distinction between guilt and shame later in this chapter, but for now know that shame can create a problem with responsibility. It can make it near impossible to apologize when it's necessary. Even minor feedback will be met with defensiveness. That's because where there is shame, there is already the belief that you're unworthy. Admitting wrongdoing, then, feels like a scary magnification of this belief.

3. *We shame.* "Shamed people, shame people" is my favorite way to put it. It describes the way we disown our shame by trying to relocate it in someone else. This helps us feel like we're escaping it.

   It's the kid at school who bullies to feel powerful because he's being bullied at home. It's the guy who denigrates his girlfriend because he feels small, and if he can make her feel small as well, he'll have more power, control, and therefore more confidence. It's the girl on social media who boasts constantly about her accomplishments and talks down to her audience. Boasting is a way of overcompensating for insecurity.

   Most of the time, however, shaming others is subtle. It's name calling, ridiculing, or expressing disgust. It's passive-aggressive behaviors such as eye rolling and turning away when you don't want to engage. Sometimes it's our use of sarcasm. Yes, sarcasm

can be a way of shaming others. Because shaming is any de-
risive mechanism we use to communicate to someone that we
wish they would think differently or act differently. It doesn't
require us to articulate our wishes or work through tension. It's
an easy, cheap way to take pressure off. It also leaves us feeling
a little bit more superior, which is, of course, the product of our
own shame.

4. *We people please.* People pleasing centers other people's goals
   and expectations in our lives. It centers their needs and wants.
   It centers their contentment and satisfaction often at the ex-
   pense of our own. We see a bit of this in both Amy's and Shavonne's story. Shame-driven people pleasing can look like

   ▶ softening our personal boundaries

   ▶ breaking promises to ourselves

   ▶ risking our own safety and protection

   ▶ disrespecting or violating our own values

   ▶ forfeiting our own goals, desires, and needs to fulfill the
     needs of someone else

   Our deep fears about who we are put us in overdrive when it
   comes to people pleasing. Our hope? That if we do everything
   right by the people in our lives, we can secure the love and affection we need. If we can just make this person see how "good"
   we are (ironically, we don't feel good about ourselves at all),
   they'll let us stay in their lives and we'll finally belong to someone.
   Nobody rejects someone who meets all their needs, right?

   Wrong. People pleasing is an illusion. It's a performance. It can't
   really secure the love that we need from people. Not in any
   meaningful way, since love that's based on what you've done,
   or how well you've done it, isn't love at all. That's a transaction.

5. *We strive for perfection*. Motivated by shame, the drive to be perfect is automatic and intense. Perfectionism and shame are two sides of the same coin. The problem with perfectionism is that what is unresolved deep down inside (I am fundamentally flawed) can't be solved quickly on the surface (look at me, I'm doing everything perfectly!). All you have is a parallel universe where one world can't affect the other.

   Perfectionism is a cover-up. In a *Super Soul Sunday* interview, the renowned shame researcher Brené Brown said it best: "Perfectionism is the cover for the fear that 'if people see what's really happening, I won't be worthy of connection and acceptance.' It's the idea that 'if I'm perfect, or do [something] perfectly, *then* I will be accepted and loved.'"

   Perfectionism acts as a defense. We believe that if we can achieve perfection, we can guard ourselves against criticism and rejection. For someone who already deals with shame, the possibility of rejection is unbearable.

   This belief leads to all-or-none thinking—"If I can't do it perfectly, why do it at all?" This, in turn, leads to self-sabotaging behavior—giving up too soon or giving up altogether before you even start. At best, you may struggle seriously with procrastination. The healthy part of you may want to start something new, but the shamed part of you is too afraid of falling short. A battle inside you ensues, and the shamed part often wins.

   The truth is, we can never be perfect. We know this at a conscious level. Neither can we completely avoid criticism at times or rejection. Such is the reality of life. The better alternative is to learn how to deal with criticism—when it's fair and when it's unfair—and how to better process rejection so you don't spiral.

6. *We "should" on ourselves*. Should statements are another way we shame ourselves. *I should be married by now. I should be*

making more money. I should have more to show for myself. I should have lost more of this weight.

Should statements are motivated by fear that we're not measuring up. They are untethered, unrealistic standards we set for ourselves that make us feel bad when we fall short. They reflect the felt gap between your actual self (who you are right now) and your ideal self (who you strive to be). It's totally okay to have an ideal self. An ideal self motivates you to reach your highest potential.

But dogging yourself for not being your ideal self yet is an avenue for shame to thrive. It's a form of self-accusation that blames your shortcomings on your fundamental defectiveness. It also won't get you any closer to your goals. Shame is demotivating. Should statements must be challenged. Two questions can help with that.

1. *Is this true? Is this should statement a true statement?* An honest look may reveal that what you're telling yourself is actually an outright lie. Or perhaps more complicated, a half-truth that you need to re-examine and shed.

2. *Why? Why "should" you do X or Y?* What happens if you don't? Is there a legitimate concern here? If so, what will motivate you to move forward? For example, instead of "should," how about "I get to," as in "I get to focus on finding love now." Or "I want to," as in "I want to be further along in my career." Or "I choose to," as in "I choose to workout today" or "I choose to skip the dessert tonight." Or "I can," as in "I can make more money in my life."

Can you feel the difference? Changing your language helps honor both where you are and where you want to go. You need language that doesn't unnecessarily rob you of your confidence.

THE CASE FOR HEALTHY SHAME?

Shame enters our lives in big and small ways, and we must pay attention to it. Its impacts are real. But is shame always harmful? Is all shame bad? We have to acknowledge that shame is an emotion God gave us the capacity to experience—albeit a painful one. For this reason, we have to consider that shame may serve a purpose, just like everything else God creates does.

In my child psychology class, we spend a good two weeks discussing the emotional and social development of infants and toddlers. This includes a day of diving into shame academically and understanding it as an important self-conscious emotion.

At about two- or three-years-old, you began to understand yourself as separate from others. You developed a sense of self. Then you became conscious of this self. You became conscious of yourself in a world that had rules, standards, and expectations. You would soon learn from your parents or caregivers that you were to follow these rules, standards, and expectations. You would learn to feel good about yourself when you did so (pride) and not so good about yourself when you did not (guilt, shame, embarrassment). And this was generally a good thing. Most of us aren't murderers, thieves, or liars for the simple fact that we learned not to be. These acts are now unfathomable to us. We would feel terrible if we did them. They defy our internalized standards of right and wrong and threaten our deep desire to remain in good standing in our relationships. Self-conscious emotions regulate these motives.

That sinking feeling we experience when we have betrayed our personal value system is the mark of shame. Healthy shame. Healthy shame emerges when we feel we have crossed an important boundary in our relationships or when our behavior breaks trust with others or ourselves. Whether it's your unfaithfulness to your spouse or the terrible words you hurled at your kids, healthy shame signals to us that something is wrong, and it drives us to make amends.

Some scholars use the word *guilt* to replace this idea of healthy shame in an attempt to relegate shame in general as wholly bad. I think this is a mistake. We have to acknowledge that in Scripture, psychological literature, and many different languages, the idea of shame is not only distinct from guilt, but it is sometimes deemed productive. We have to consider that shame, too, has an adaptive purpose. Let's look more closely at their distinctions.

Healthy shame versus guilt. Guilt is the feeling of responsibility or remorse for some offense, crime, or wrongdoing. This can be real or imagined. Shame is the painful feeling that arises from our consciousness of wrongdoing. It is the awareness of something dishonorable or improper, done by oneself or another. The key distinction here is the focus.

Guilt's focus is the effect of our actions on somebody else. Its pain comes from the awareness that our actions have caused harm or injury. But shame's focus is on what our actions (or someone else's actions toward us) may say about ourselves. Shame reflects an awareness of what we've come to believe that we are.

Psychotherapist Dr. Joseph Burgo shares a helpful personal example of this distinction in an article.

> I once said something hurtful at a dinner party, and on some level, I intended it to be hurtful. Afterward, I felt guilty because I could see that I had hurt my friend. More painfully, I also felt ashamed that I was the sort of person who would behave that way. Guilt arose as a result of inflicting pain on somebody else; I felt shame in relation to myself.[1]

The realization that you are "the type of person" to do something is an important one. It's a healthy one. Part of what makes healthy shame healthy is that it shows us our limits. We are not perfect. We are not better than anyone else. And we all stumble and fall short of the glory of God (Romans 3:23).

I would argue that healthy shame is what Peter felt when he denied Christ, though he swore he never would. In Matthew 26:33-35, when Jesus foreshadows his death and tells his disciples that they too will soon reject him, Peter says: "Even if all fall away on account of you, I never will!" In fact, Peter feels so strongly and so sure about his love and loyalty to Christ that he affirms his promise once again in the very next verse: "Even if I have to die with you, I will never disown you."

But then push comes to shove and Jesus is taken. Peter is spotted, and he is questioned three times. Verses 74-75 tell us what happens after the third:

> Then [Peter] began to call down curses, and he swore to them, "I don't know the man!"
>
> Immediately a rooster crowed. Then Peter remembered the word Jesus had spoken: "Before the rooster crows, you will disown me three times." And he went outside and wept bitterly.

I imagine Peter's bitter tears were about coming to terms with his own humanity. I imagine he was confronting the reality that he was in fact the type of person to betray his leader and his best friend. I imagine it was hard for him to face himself at that moment. I imagine his pain and disappointment.

The best thing about Peter's story, however, is that it didn't end there. Jesus didn't allow Peter to stay in his shame. That wouldn't have been purposeful. That wouldn't have been healthy either. In John 21, we find Jesus post-resurrection with his disciples and Peter again, being the amazing counselor that he is. We find him re-creating a tough moment in Peter's life—his three-time denial of Jesus—to give Peter, it seems, a chance to get it right. Jesus confronts Peter and asks him, "Do you love me?" Peter of course says yes. But Jesus didn't ask this once, or twice. He asked this three times. Each time, Peter was allowed to reaffirm his love for Christ. Coincidence? I think not.

Healthy shame versus toxic shame. Healthy shame brings us back to relationship. Toxic shame cuts us off from it. This is the ultimate distinction. And this is the enemy's plan for us. That we feel so badly about ourselves that we hide. That we feel so badly about ourselves that we shift blame and denigrate others. That we feel so badly about ourselves that we trade in the real work of healing ourselves for unsustainable Band-Aids in the form of people pleasing and perfection. Let's be clear about the differences.

Healthy shame creates pause in our life and relationships—to reassess, make changes, and re-engage when appropriate. Toxic shame drives us to cut ourselves off from important opportunities and relationships.

Healthy shame humbles us. It makes us aware of our limitations and inspires compassion for ourselves and others. Toxic shame demoralizes us. It causes us to lose hope and confidence in ourselves and to expect the bare minimum.

Healthy shame accepts forgiveness from God and others. It embraces new beginnings. Toxic shame plays our failures over and over again in our heads like a broken record.

Healthy shame leads to improved functioning. Toxic shame leads to anxiety, insecurity, depression, and dysfunction.

Healthy shame brings us back to God. Toxic shame—the belief that we are fundamentally wrong, irreversibly damaged, and unworthy of belonging—is where the enemy wants us to stay.

THE HOUSE THAT BUILT SHAME

Childhood trauma and shame. If you've been the victim of physical, sexual, or emotional abuse or bullying, or of neglect, abandonment, or any kind of family violence, chances are you've battled shame your whole life. *Trauma transfers shame.*

When we are kids, we blame ourselves for things that happen to us. No matter how much we hear "it wasn't your fault," the need to find a reason, and therefore make sense of the pain, is too great. *If it's not my fault then whose is it?* Feeling small, defenseless, and powerless makes it difficult to point the finger at anyone else. It is much easier to take the blame and just accept it. The blame is internalized and carried into adulthood. It becomes our automatic rationalization for bad behavior and bad circumstances. *It's my fault we broke up. It's my fault my children are behaving so poorly. It's my fault everything around me is falling apart.*

Childhood trauma causes us to take the shame that belonged to the people who harmed us and make it our own. The vulnerability and dependability in childhood makes us easily subject to the shame from those whose behavior is shameful.

Unspoken family rules and shame. You also grew up with a set of family rules. Rules that came from your parents that included the influence of your culture and religious tradition. Some of these rules helped your family run smoothly—where to put your shoes, when to come home at night, what chores you have to do. But there were other rules, more important rules, that taught you how to *be*. These were the rules of engagement. They taught you how to deal with other family members, other people, and yourself. These rules weren't always clear or explicit, but they were certainly felt and understood.

These are the rules you may need to look back at if you find yourself struggling with shame. For example, what were you taught about success and failure? What was implicitly or explicitly conveyed to you? Was it to share and celebrate your successes in life but hide or cower after failure? If so, you likely learned that failure is deeply shameful, that you should feel really bad when you fail, and that you're probably not much to look at when you do.

Here are things you can ask yourself as you reflect on the rules that you learned.

- What were you taught about sex and intimacy?
- What were you taught about trust or love?

- What were you taught about personal boundaries?

- What were you taught about food, weight, and fitness?

- What were you taught about money?

- What were you taught about your emotions? What were you taught about tears and vulnerability? What did it mean to be "strong"?

- What were you taught about making mistakes?

- Could people in your family say "I'm sorry"?

- What were you taught about God?

A good look at your family rules might help you better understand your shame.

Shame on demand. Toxic shame doesn't just happen in childhood. It happens in the big and small interactions of our adult lives as well. Shame can happen in the kitchen, at the dinner table, or in the bedroom. Shame can happen in the backyard or in the backseat. Shame can happen in the classroom, the boardroom, or the audition room. Shame can happen in a text or an email. Shame can happen on Instagram.

Shame can also happen through strangers. In 2005, my college roommate and I took a trip to Palm Springs with the men we were currently dating. My roommate was dating a Mexican American, but the rest of us were Black. One afternoon we got hungry and decided to walk to lunch. We had no idea what was about to happen to us at a crosswalk. While we were standing, waiting, joking around with each other, two men drove by in their car, yelled the N-word repeatedly at us, and threw their fountain drinks at our faces. They were gone before we could fight back. Literally stunned to silence, none of us said a word the rest of the walk. In fact, I remember it being hours before any of us could say a word. That day shame happened at a crosswalk, compliments of two racist men in a Corvette.

Shame can happen in any of our interactions, at any time or any place. If in these moments a sense of smallness came over you, that was probably shame. Note that the goal here isn't to find blame for the sake of blame. That isn't productive. The goal is to go back to where your shame came from so you can unpack it and make it stop.

OUR NEED FOR RADICAL LOVE

Since shame is a problem with how we view ourselves fundamentally, we need something that can fundamentally transform our views. Something powerful, something strong, and something that can transcend. May I suggest to you that what we need is love. Radical love.

Look at the definition of *radical*: affecting the fundamental nature of something; far-reaching or thorough. And love? Well love has a million definitions, but one of my favorites of all time is one I heard once in a trauma seminar and will never forget: "Love is listening to people's stories and retelling it in the way they've never heard it before."

As a healing professional who knows firsthand the importance of sitting with people in their stories, in their pain, and in their shame, and reflecting back the sheer beauty, power, and strength that's become of them, I can't stress enough how important this way of loving somebody is.

If I could define radical love, then, I would say that it's being so committed to seeing someone in a way they've yet to see that it eventually and ultimately transforms them fundamentally. Radical love is about seeing, acknowledging, and affirming our divine, glorious nature. *Radical love heals radical shame.*

THE RADICAL LOVE OF GOD

God's love is radical. We've seen how God's love cuts through shame countless times in the Bible—the story where Jesus met with the Samaritan woman at the well (John 4), the story where he stopped everything to heal the woman who'd been bleeding for twelve years

(Luke 8), the story where he told accusers of a woman caught in adultery to cast the first stone (John 8), and many more. But his radical love isn't reserved for them or for back then. It's for you and me too.

God's radical love must be encountered. This can happen in a few different ways, but it always involves God's presence. You can't encounter something you're not in the midst of. The good news is, God won't ever withhold himself from us. As we draw near, he draws near. His love is always accessible. His healing presence is on demand.

Sometimes we'll encounter God's loving presence directly. We'll see it spiritually or feel it supernaturally. A lot of times, we'll experience it through people. Through the individuals in our lives who are devoted to loving us and committed to seeing us grow and heal. But all the time, we can encounter God through worship. I find this incredibly empowering. With worship, we can encounter God's radical love whenever we want.

In my studies of worship in Scripture, I've come to define it as the reflection, contemplation, acknowledgment, engagement, celebration, elevation, and adoration of the truth of God. Worship is a heart-grasp of who God truly is. What makes worship so healing, however, is that as we worship God, we also get a heart-grasp of who we are to him. This is what we need. This is what our shame needs.

Nineteenth-century English poet William Blake once said, "We become what we behold." And isn't that the truth. As we behold in worship the truth of God's love for us, the truth of his grace and forgiveness, the truth of his plans for our lives, and the truth of our belovedness to him, these truths begin to hold more weight and anchor us. They begin to reflect in our lives as the untruths we've been recycling in our hearts and minds diminish in comparison. Whatever we feed in ourselves grows, while whatever we starve shrinks.

To be clear, we can worship God in a few different ways. Hebrews 13:15 points out one way: "Through Jesus, therefore, let us continually offer to God a sacrifice of praise—the fruit of lips that openly profess his name."

Professing God's name with the fruit of our lips is something many of us already do at our church services, in our cars, and with our small groups and friends. This is good. We've likely already experienced the healing worship brings.

But the science of this kind of worship is also worth noting. As one example, a study conducted by Swedish researchers monitored the heart rates of members of a choir. What they found was incredible. As the choir members sang in unison, their heart rates synchronized. Their pulses began to rise and fall at the same time. In other words, their worship caused their hearts to beat as one.

Since shame's main goal is to tell us that we are unworthy of belonging, then what can be more healing than sharing the same heartbeat? Encountering God through worship is a radical act. It has the power to transform us from the inside out. If worship isn't a part of your life, I suggest that you make it so. If it already is, I suggest that you drive it up even more.

TOOLS FOR SHEDDING SHAME

As we begin or continue to pursue an encounter with radical love, we gain more authority in our healing. We can work in accordance with the efforts of God to heal us. Shame must be called out of our lives, and how we view ourselves must be repaired.

Name the shame. Shame festers in silence and secrecy. It thrives and diversifies in the dark. When it hooks its claws into you, it hopes that you won't say anything, because once you do, shame's hold on you loosens. As Brené Brown puts it: "shame cannot survive being spoken." She's absolutely right.

For this reason, it's important that you recognize the covert ways that shame operates in your life. It's important that you look closely at your hiding, or difficulty taking responsibility, or subtle shaming of others, or people pleasing, or drive for perfection, and consider that these are symptoms of a deeper issue.

Once you recognize your shame, call it out for what it is. Get it out of hiding and out in the open. This doesn't mean you need to scream it from the rooftops (you're certainly welcome to if you'd like), but it does mean you need to make it plain to see. This could mean starting with a journal entry—writing down your true, most vulnerable feelings about yourself and acknowledging the results of these beliefs—or opening up with a trusted friend. This could mean talking with a therapist, since they are trained to reflect back to you the real you. Whatever method you choose, decide now that you will no longer keep your shame a secret. Naming your shame loosens the grip shame has on you and opens yourself up to a different view.

I love what this looked like for Shavonne, who found new grace in an old story.

Looking back, I've learned to see victory in my story. My mother did break the chain of addiction off her life before she died. My aunt took me in at a dark time and raised me to be a strong, intelligent, God-fearing woman. The seed once growing in my belly became a kind, loving, intelligent young man and is my everyday reminder that "in all things, God works for the good of those who love him." I look back on these things and I am filled with pride. The events of my past will always be a part of who I am, but not for the shame it brought. They are badges of honor and resilience. They are reminders of God's incredible love for me. They are reminders that he has always had his hand on my life.

Seek reparative relationship. Since most of our shame comes from old experiences, healing our shame requires new experiences. New experiences that will help us write new narratives for our lives. This is the stuff of reparative relationship.

A reparative relationship helps restore your dignity. Dignity is the state or quality of being worthy of honor and respect. Thus, restoring dignity means engaging with someone in a way that communicates that inherent worthiness of honor and respect. Practically speaking, this looks like a relationship that, either in word or action, is characterized by:

- *Commitment:* You are worth me sitting down and talking to. You are worth me listening. You are worth the time, the energy, and the effort.

- *Empathy and compassion:* Oh, that is painful. This is awful. I can imagine what that feels like. I have felt like this before. Me too.

- *Curiosity, awe, and wonder:* Wow! How did you get through that? What was that like? How were you able to do that?

- *Validation:* You make sense. Your feelings make sense. I can understand why you feel this way.

- *Affirmation:* I see you. I see your worth and value. I see God in you.

Though dignity is a big, grand deal, it happens in small moments. Just like shame. We are repaired by words, sentiments, actions, and interactions. We are restored by small but powerful moments that ultimately communicate that there is nothing fundamentally wrong with us. There is nothing we could do to make us unworthy of love. Neither is there anything we can do that would strip away our inherent value. Our worth and value is rooted in God's love, and there is nothing that can separate us from it (Romans 8:31-39). Not our past, trauma, failures, or shortcomings. God's love dignifies us the most.

We can be intentional about creating reparative relationships with one another. As you become conscious of what you need from your partner, family, friends, or leaders, you can communicate those needs. You can share your struggles with shame and ask that the people who love you offer you more empathy, curiosity, or validation. In turn, as you learn what inherent worth and value looks and feels like, you'll be able to see it more in others and return the favor. Fostering this kind of relationship takes work, but it's possible.

Inspired self-love. The intentional, reparative relationship we seek to develop with another is no more important than the relationship we develop with ourselves. You are with people, sometimes. You are with yourself always. You may not always be able to get what you need from people, but you can always give what you need back to yourself. Self-love can transform us . . . and does.

First Corinthians 13:4-7 is a popular blueprint for love. It reads:

> Love is patient, love is kind. It does not envy, it does not boast, it is not proud. It does not dishonor others, it is not self-seeking, it is not easily angered, it keeps no record of wrongs. Love does not delight in evil but rejoices with the truth. It always protects, always trusts, always hopes, always perseveres.

But how far and wide can we apply this? Can this love be a model for how we love ourselves? I say yes. When God commands us to love him with our whole heart and also love our neighbors as ourselves (Matthew 22:36-40), he's certainly not telling us to treat our neighbors like trash. There's an assumption and an expectation that we love ourselves well enough for it to be a model for how we love others. We should love ourselves no more or no less than others, and in both instances, this love should be quality love. When we keep this in mind, 1 Corinthians takes on new meaning. We get a clearer picture of what treating ourselves with love looks like. Take a look with me.

Treating ourselves with love means being patient. It means giving ourselves time to heal, grow, and "get it right."

Treating ourselves with love means extending kindness. We are gentle and sweet to ourselves and considerate of our needs.

Treating ourselves with love means rejecting envy. It means we look inward and focus on our own enoughness.

Treating ourselves with love means rejecting boastfulness and arrogance, and practicing humility. It means learning to see significance in ourselves without needing to feel superior.

Treating ourselves with love means honoring others. We begin to see in others the inherent worthiness we see in ourselves.

Treating ourselves with love means being forgiving and forbearing in our own lives. It means we don't make snap judgments, rage, or easily give up on who we are becoming.

Treating ourselves with love means letting go of our past mistakes. It means giving ourselves a fresh start when we need it.

Treating ourselves with love means celebrating the truth about who we are. This truth is encountered in God.

Treating ourselves with love means protecting ourselves from unnecessary harm. It means establishing reasonable boundaries to guard our heart, mind, and body, as well as our joy, freedom, and peace.

Treating ourselves with love means trusting and believing in ourselves, and persevering.

In Amy's story, shame came on the heels of the gynecologist's diagnosis. Healing required that she accepted the love of God and also learned to love herself.

The months after my doctor's visit were difficult. Daily I had a reminder that I couldn't trust myself. Daily I had a reminder that I broke a promise I'd made to myself and to God. I felt like a huge disappointment. But with the encouragement of a few friends, I turned back to God for a new way to look at the situation. Quiet meditations on the Word and worship turned to deeper convictions. It wasn't over for me. I wasn't damaged goods. I was still worthy of love and affection. I made a decision then to stop railing on myself and instead practice self-compassion. I would be patient with myself in learning how I could make good decisions for myself and choose better. I would fully accept God's forgiveness, and I would also forgive myself. There doesn't seem to be much room for an intimate relationship with both God and shame.

WHEN AND HOW TO FIND THERAPY

Nothing will work unless you do.

MAYA ANGELOU

All great changes are preceded by chaos.

DEEPAK CHOPRA

When we talk about our feelings, they become less overwhelming, less upsetting, and less scary.

FRED ROGERS

The secret to change is to focus all of your energy, not on fighting the old, but on building the new.

DAN MILLMAN

And you? When will you begin the long journey into yourself?

RUMI

WHEN SHOULD I SPEAK
TO A PROFESSIONAL?

If you were to pose this question to any expert or advocate of mental health, you will get some standard answers. Seek therapy if you're noticing symptoms of depressions, anxiety, or any other distressing mental health concern. Seek therapy if the mental or emotional concerns you're having are starting to negatively impact your life, relationships, and work. Seek therapy if you've experienced trauma or deep grief. Definitely seek therapy if you notice you're thinking more about dying or contemplating taking your life.

I would give you the same answers. These are crucial concerns, and we all could benefit from some additional support during these times.

But these aren't the only reasons I want you to seek therapy. I want you to seek therapy for many more. I want you to seek therapy because there's pain or frustration somewhere. The pain or frustration that drew you to this book. I want you to seek therapy because you don't have to work out your hurt, discouragement, anxiety, insecurity, envy, or shame alone. I want you to seek therapy because there are a hundred ways therapy can serve you, strengthen you, and better your life and relationships. I believe wholeheartedly this is what you deserve.

It just so happens that I recently conducted a brief survey with my students. I asked whether they've sought therapy in the past year and, if so, why they did. With their permission, I've included the responses of twenty-seven students. All real and all worthy:

1. I sought therapy to help me gain a sense of control amid the chaos in my life.

2. I sought therapy because I knew my current coping mechanisms weren't working.

3. I sought therapy to heal my depression. I was tired of feeling alone and helpless.

4. I'm going to therapy because my boyfriend is concerned about the way I deal with my feelings.

5. I'm going to therapy because I'm bitter and angry. I can't get over what happened to me.

6. I sought therapy to help me control my anxiety.

7. I'm going to therapy to get a better handle on my emotions.

8. I sought therapy to control my social anxiety. It's ruining my life.

9. I sought therapy to gain control of my thoughts.

10. I'm going to therapy to help me overcome my fear of abandonment that I think started after my parents' divorce.

11. I sought therapy because I witnessed lots of abuse when I was a kid.

12. I sought therapy to work on my self-esteem.

13. I'm going to therapy because I hate my life.

14. I sought therapy to figure out why I couldn't get over my ex.

15. I sought therapy to work on my fear of rejection. It paralyzes me.

16. I sought therapy to figure out why I'm so short-tempered.

17. I sought therapy for my ADHD symptoms.

18. I'm going to family therapy to help me better understand my son.

19. I sought therapy to help me forgive my father.

20. My mother was diagnosed with bipolar disorder, and I sought therapy to help me deal with her abuse.

21. I've been in therapy since tenth grade. My mom died of cancer, and I needed to work out my grief. Now I'm working on attachment issues.

22. I sought therapy to deal with my parents' divorce.

23. I sought therapy to break the cycle I have with dating emotionally unavailable men.

24. I sought therapy because my family was falling apart. My grades were suffering. I couldn't make myself happy anymore.

25. I sought therapy to cope with the loss of my mom. Grief was spilling everywhere into my life.

26. I sought therapy because I don't have any friends.

27. I sought therapy because I'm lonely. But I'm tired of getting hurt.

There are many reasons to seek therapy. Probably as many reasons as there are individual stories. If you can stand to be healthier, happier, or freer, therapy is for you.

WHO SHOULD I SEE?

Before you begin your search, it'll help to know what you're looking for. It'll help to know who's who in the great, big world of mental health professionals. Here's a nonexhaustive list of the most commonly used clinicians you'll find.

Psychiatrists (MD). Psychiatrists are medical doctors. They attended medical school and then completed a four-year specialty in psychiatry. Their medical background is what qualifies them legally to prescribe medications to treat mental illness, and they are the only mental health professional who can. They are also trained to apply the use of evidence-based psychotherapy (talk therapy), but their work typically places a primary, or at least equal, focus on pharmacotherapy (use of drugs) as it does these other methods. Sometimes psychiatrists work alongside psychologists to treat serious mental illnesses (e.g., major depression, bipolar disorder) if that's what the client needs, wants, or requests.

Psychologists. Psychologists are not medical doctors but have obtained doctoral degrees (PsyD, PhD) that took them anywhere from five to ten years of training and practice. Their specialty is treating individuals with mental disorders (e.g., depression, bipolar disorder, anxiety, eating disorders) or "almost" disorders through the use of psychotherapy only. They are also trained to treat children, adolescents, couples, and family-related issues and individual concerns that are not necessarily related to a mental disorder. And they are trained to provide testing, for example, if you want to get tested for ADHD, personality functioning, or the severity of your disorder. In short, psychologists are trained to treat everybody and anybody, using any number of psychotherapies, and may clarify their specialty in their bio or introduction. For what it's worth, I trained as a clinical psychologist and also see a clinical psychologist as needed. I'm clearly a fan of the work.

Licensed Marriage and Family Therapists (LMFT). Marriage and family therapists are master's-level professionals with training just a few years shy of psychologists. However, their training is quite robust, and their work often overlaps with that of a psychologist. MFTs are known for their primary focus on healthy relationships, hence marriage and families. The focus is what's key. Whether an MFT is treating an individual (which they do) or the whole family, the primary focus is the "system"—the coupleship, marriage, family, group, work setting, and so on, that is contributing to the problem or concerns. The general idea is that if you can change one part of the system, you can change the whole thing.

Licensed Professional Clinical Counselor (LPCC) and Licensed Mental Health Counselor (LMHC). Professional clinical counselors and mental health counselors are also master's-level professionals, but their focus is broader than that of the LMFT. They are trained to assess problems and use a variety of therapy techniques. They are perhaps best used to support personal development and growth, and to assist individuals in a time of crisis, support, and adjustment to disability, among other psychosocial issues. The difference between the two is generally just the state in which they were licensed. States have different names for different clinical degrees and licenses.

Licensed Clinical Social Worker (LCSW). Clinical social workers are master's-level professionals who are trained to provide counseling services, but counseling is just one tool of many they use to help people with a broad range of issues. Clinical social workers are masters at connecting their clients to public and private assistance programs that can provide housing, poverty relief, food assistance, job training, employment resources, medical services, and protections against violence, among other things. If needs are varied, clinical social workers can be a great fit.

Pastoral counselors, Christian counselors, Christian therapists, and spiritually integrated therapists. Lots of church people look for Christian mental health professionals. The reasons are self-explanatory. However, it's important to know if your Christian counselor of choice is actually licensed to provide proper psychotherapy. If they are, they will have an MD, PsyD, PhD, LMFT, LPCC, LSW, or LMHC next to their name, or in a few states be licensed as a pastoral counselor (LPC). The degree and license confirm they have gone through the adequate, science-backed training to treat your disorders, traumas, and relationship issues, and either personally or academically have the background to provide spiritual guidance as well.

If they do not have these letters, they are not nationally recognized as mental health professionals. They may be certified to provide counsel by an unrecognized or state-specific governing body, however. Or they may be claiming to provide psychotherapy regardless, and that's illegal.

Legal issues aside, a nonlicense does not mean a person can't be helpful to you. They can be—especially if this counselor is operating in a safe setting and you trust them and their work. A pastor or priest with no clinical training is a great example of this. They don't claim to be therapists, but they can listen, utilize tools, and provide guidance, encouragement, and support. Sometimes this is all you need. Other times, you'll need more. Hopefully you and your pastor can work honestly enough to know when a true mental health professional is more suitable for your needs.

How much does all of this matter? Not *that* much. I mean, it matters in the sense that you should be sure that you're working with a licensed individual and that you're getting exactly what you want from the experience. But what matters most in your healing won't be the specific mix of letters next to the person's name; it will be the relationship. It will be the trust. It will be the quality of support and care you feel they provide you. After all is said and done, is this the professional you feel you can believe in? Do they help you believe in yourself? You'll have to try them out and see.

CAN I AFFORD THIS?

Yes, you can.

Some of you have insurance that covers mental health services and will have affordable copays. Some of your employers may even have Employment Assistance Programs (EAP) that will allow you free or discounted sessions. Check with your employer.

But most of you don't have mental health coverage (or any good coverage for any good therapist anyway) or any such setup with your employer. You'll have to pay out of pocket. Rest assured that there are many affordable options for you.

For one, many psychotherapists work on a sliding scale: this means they will work with you based on your income needs. Depending on the city you live in, a typical sliding scale may look like $70 to $150 per hour. This will vary on your location, however, and you'll need to just call and ask. I've gotten quotes for $300 per hour and also for $65. Both from private practitioners. Prices tend to vary by cities, towns, and neighborhoods, and some clinicians know they can get away with a lot. (Not that it's not worth the investment.)

If around $70 a session is still too much for you, there are even cheaper options. Community centers, university centers, and training centers are known for their incredibly low prices. The difference is that you'll likely be working with a therapy trainee who is working closely with a licensed clinician. This means that they have done enough schooling to start practicing but are meeting with their supervisors to ensure the quality of their service. If you don't mind the chain of command, you get quality care for less than $15 per hour or even free! Since my suggestion is that you interview and consult with any professional you are interested in seeing, it certainly doesn't hurt to try this route and see if it works for you.

HOW DO I FIND THEM?

Referrals are easiest. You can ask your general physician if they have any mental health professional recommendations for you. You can also ask friends and family if they've worked with anyone helpful. You would still need to do your own interviewing and consulting with them, and we'll talk about this next, but at least you'll have a quick place to start.

If you've asked around and there are no suggestions, remember that you are living in the mighty internet age and everything you need to know is at your fingers. Google won't let you down. Here are some very simple steps you can take:

Search "therapist near me." Or, if you like, a more specific request, such as "family counseling near me," "MFT near me," "Christian therapist near me," "affordable counseling near me," "Spanish-speaking therapist near me."

Visit a few of the web pages that come up. The first couple of suggestions are likely to be psychologytoday.com, goodtherapy.org, or betterhelp.com (they've definitely got strong marketing teams!), and they are all great starting places. But you can scroll through a page or two to give you confidence that in the end you did a solid search. Once you land on a page, type in any necessary filtering information and pull up a list of therapists.

Skim the personal summaries under the therapists you see. These are short paragraphs that detail the therapist's degree and licenses (PsyD, LMFT, LPCC, etc.), their approach to therapy, and their specialties. Consider whether gender, race, or the age of the therapist matters to you. You might be able to tell all of these things from their photos if they included one. Your overall goal is to get a quick sense of whether or not this person could be helpful to you. With so much information, it will be easy to get overwhelmed, but don't. Just skim and skip along and trust that you'll find what you need.

Create a list of five therapists. This is an arbitrary number, but I want this process to feel manageable to you. You'll need to call each of these therapists, so you don't want to go overboard. Start with a small number and save their contact information.

Prepare your consultation. Once you're able to make contact with your potential therapist, you'll want to maximize the short time you have. This conversation is what will help you decide who you want to try and sit with. Some therapists may offer free first-time sessions, but most will create just enough time on a call to get a sense of what you're looking for. Prepare for your first contact by putting some thought into the following questions:

- Why do I want to go to therapy? What issues do I want to work out?

- What kind of approach do I want my therapist to take? (If you don't know, that's okay. You'll be able to ask about their approach and see if that resonates with you.)

- What is my weekly/monthly budget for this?

- How far am I willing to drive for therapy? Do I want in-person sessions or tele-sessions?

Call each therapist on your list. You'll likely get a voicemail. Leave a message asking for a return call.

WHAT DO I ASK? INTERVIEWING
YOUR POTENTIAL THERAPIST

The next step is the most important. You'll need to conduct an "interview" of sorts and get a sense if this is someone you want to connect with personally. Once you make that initial contact, here are some questions you can ask the therapist:

- How do you work? What's your approach?

- What experience do you have treating my issues?

- What are your fees? Do you work on a sliding scale?

- What's your availability?

- I'm a _____. How do you feel about working with that?

This last question has a blank because we sometimes have unique needs or requests. For example, in my last search for a therapist, it was important to me that the psychologist I chose was comfortable and confident working with a fellow doctor in psychology. I wanted someone highly experienced, obviously, and someone who wouldn't back down in any way because I would essentially know, objectively speaking, as much as they did. So in my interview that was one of the first things I shared. What things do you really want your therapist to understand about you? Your heritage? Your background? Your work? Your faith? Share it and see how they respond.

Your job with this interview is to feel out the vibe. Is there a connection? Do you feel like they might be able to help you? Do you feel like you'll be comfortable with them? Are they giving you a price you're willing or able to pay? Does their availability work for you?

If you can answer yes to these questions, book your first session! A good call is a good first sign, but a good first session is what will seal the deal. So start the process. If you get into the therapy room and things click, commit to working with this therapist for at least a few months and seeing how you do. If in the first session nothing clicks, finish the session with grace and don't return. Depending on the situation, you can leave a voicemail or send an email notifying them of your decision, or you can just not follow-up. On to the next!

WHAT CAN I EXPECT? HOW WILL
I KNOW IF IT'S WORKING?

Some of what you expect will depend on the approach that your therapist uses. However, expect forty-five- to fifty-minute sessions once a week (unless you agree to more or less frequent sessions). Expect that your first couple of sessions will prioritize getting a sense of what you need, where you've struggled, and any personal or family history that may add context to your concerns. Also expect that everything you talk about with your therapist will remain confidential unless you report, indicate, or suggest that you are in danger of hurting yourself or others. Expect a process and a journey.

Expect it to work. I say this knowing full well that some things don't work. You should definitely pay attention to how you're feeling, how you're bonding with your therapist, and if you're growing over time. But a positive, expectant attitude, as we all know, goes a long way. Plus you want to give this therapy chapter a chance. Sometimes therapy immediately makes you feel like things are going to get better. Sometimes it gets more difficult first, and then better. Sometimes you'll leave inspired; sometimes you'll leave annoyed. The key is that you feel connected and cared for, like you're gaining insight and understanding, and you feel, at least within a few months, that things are shifting, however small. Real progress takes time.

THE NIGHT SHINES LIKE DAY

W<small>E STARTED OUR JOURNEY TOGETHER</small> with an accepting embrace of who we are. It's only fitting that we end it with an embrace of who God is.

Out of the many beautiful things I've learned and experienced about God, one of my absolute favorite things to hold on to is the way God sees our pain. Yes, God is certainly compassionate toward our emotional suffering. But he doesn't quite see it the way we do.

This revelation comes from Psalm 139. It's a chapter in Scripture that I first fell in love with during my college years. It's the gift that keeps on giving. Every year, God shows me something new in it. And every time he shows me, I find new hope for an old need. I hope it can bring some comfort to you too. Let's focus now on Psalm 139:11-12. It reads:

> If I say, "Surely the darkness will hide me
>   and the light become night around me,"
> even the darkness will not be dark to you;
>   the night will shine like the day,
>   for darkness is as light to you.

The common thread of our hurt, heartbreak, trauma, discouragement, anxiety, depression, envy, and shame is that it points to some kind of darkness in our lives.

Darkness in our past, in our present, or darkness we fear is waiting for us in the future.

The darkness of failed marriages, broken families, and hurting children.

The darkness of a lost sense of meaning, purpose, or personal significance in our lives.

The darkness of pain in our bodies or pain in our hearts.

The darkness in the habits, patterns, and addictions we've tried to break, but we have found our efforts futile.

The darkness that comes with grief after losing the things most important to us.

The darkness that comes from traumatic memories at the hands of those who were supposed to love and protect us.

The darkness that hides in our thoughts and the corners of our minds.

Our tough emotions are signs of dark times. And darkness is bewildering. It's overwhelming and overburdening. It's maddening and distressing. It leaves us feeling helpless and hopeless, lost and confused. In such times, it's hard to know which way to turn or how to move forward. We just want relief, and it feels cruel sometimes that we can't just turn our emotions off. Dark times are tough times.

But our dark times aren't dark to God. Darkness doesn't change who God is in our lives, neither does it preclude his plans for us. Darkness doesn't overwhelm, bewilder, or trip him up. In fact, he's crystal clear.

God knows the pain that people in your life have caused you and sees clearly how he will restore and redeem you and cause it all to work for your good (Romans 8:28).

God knows the justice owed to you. He's acutely aware of it and sees clearly how and when he will execute it (Luke 18:7).

God knows the hearts that wish you harm, the people trying to block you or break you, and he's working a plan to prepare a table for you in front of them (Psalm 23:5). Like Joseph, what the enemy intended against you, God will use for good (Genesis 50:20).

God knows the career that will open up for you. And he sees the small opening in the window through which he will lead you.

God knows the person out there praying and waiting to marry you. And he sees how he's going to bring you two to each other.

God knows the names of the children he will fill your loving home with. And he sees how and when he will bring them into your life.

God knows the connections you need to take your life to the next level. And he sees through the quagmire and will set up your steps.

God knows the way out of your depression.

God knows the way out of your family's history of illness and addiction.

God knows the way out of generational bondage. In fact, you might be the one he's using to reverse it.

God knows the way out of crises and pandemics.

God knows the way out of all of it. All he's asking is that you hang on.

As you put to work the wisdom and instruction of God, and as you take to heart the counsel of therapists, spiritual leaders, and friends, may your knowledge of God give you some kind of hope in your distress. What we don't know, God knows. What we can't see, God sees. Darkness is but a perception. The light isn't at the end of the tunnel. It's inside it. Shining like the day.

ACKNOWLEDGMENTS

To my father Gilbert, my mother Debbie, my sister Ndidi, and my brothers Freddie and Chinedu, thank you for being my rock. It was your love, support, and encouragement that allowed me to complete this book. Your jokes helped too.

To the women who shared your heartfelt stories in this book, thank you for your transparency and vulnerability. May you continue to lead your families and communities with strength and hope, and may your journeys inspire deep faith in many.

SMALL GROUP DISCUSSION GUIDE

CHAPTER 1—THE DANGER OF SPIRITUAL BYPASSING

1. **The Antiwork of Spiritual Bypassing.** Has your pain ever been spiritually bypassed? How did it affect you? Why do you think spiritual bypassing happens often in the church?

2. **Emotions Reflect God in Us.** Reflect on the emotionality of God. What does this mean to you? How does this impact your view of your own emotions?

3. **Emotions Draw Us Back to God.** Discuss a time when an emotion that persisted in your life drew you back to God. What was the outcome?

4. **Dealing, Healing, and Moving Through.** How did the six-part framework for healing affect your view and understanding of your own healing journey? Is there something in your life that you're still healing from?

CHAPTER 2—UNCOVERING OUR CORE BELIEFS

1. **The Rise of Core Beliefs.** Recall a difficult experience in childhood. Did you internalize some beliefs from that period? Discuss.

2. **A Biblical Case for the Unconscious?** What new insights did you develop from your reflection on Dr. Piper's words and on Matthew 15:18?

3. **Uncovering Core Beliefs.** If you're comfortable, discuss your responses to the questions used to help uncover some of your core beliefs. Use the follow-up questions where you can.

4. **Core Belief Checklist.** Work through the Core Belief Checklist. How was this for you? In which categories did your core beliefs fall? Did you develop any new insights?

5. **The Question of Positive Affirmations.** "New beliefs require new experiences." How did this land for you? What ideas come to mind for seeking or creating new experiences for yourself?

CHAPTER 3—TRAUMA: OUR NEED TO TELL OUR STORY

1. **Types of Traumatic Experiences.** As a group, gain a sense of how common trauma is in our lives. Without sharing details (unless you'd like to), share whether you, or someone in your family of origin, has experienced any of these traumas.

2. **When Those Who Are Supposed to Love You Wound You.** How does the reflection on Ezekiel 34 land for you? What are you hearing God say to you about your story?

3. **What's Your Story?** What new insights did you develop about the elements of a trauma story? If you have not yet, are you ready to share your story with someone? If so, who?

4. **Finding Purpose in Pain.** How did the distinction between reason and purpose land for you? Do you see a difference? Discuss.

5. **Finding Purpose in Pain.** Can you think of a time where you have found purpose in pain? Is there something in your life now that you're seeking purpose for? Discuss.

6. **The Question of Forgiveness.** "Forgiveness is a decision you make to let go of what's owed to you." Discuss what this means to you.

CHAPTER 4—HURT: OUR NEED TO
RECOVER WHAT'S LOST

1. **The Ways We Hurt.** Get a sense of who's feeling what in the group. Share which of the ways we hurt—words, rejection, disappointment, heartbreak—you have been most wounded by. If they've all contributed significantly to your emotional pain, share which of the ways you have been most wounded by recently.

2. **The Ways We Hurt.** What new insights did you develop about any of the different ways we hurt? What should be helpful in your healing journey?

3. **Hurt by God/God, Where Are You?** Have you ever felt hurt by God? Discuss. How does your reflection on Psalm 34:18 speak into this?

4. **Self-Soothing.** How did the five-step process of self-soothing fit for you? Are you willing to try these methods and see if they would be helpful? Who comes to mind as a "soothing sponsor" for you?

5. **Emotional Unpacking.** Recall a recent hurtful experience and emotionally unpack it. Specifically, what thoughts occurred that need to be shaken? What thoughts do you want to keep? What's going back into your new suitcase?

CHAPTER 5—DISCOURAGEMENT: OUR NEED
FOR CONFIDENCE AND COURAGE

1. **Hannah's Hope.** In what ways have you felt like Hannah? What in your life have you hoped or worked for "year after year"? Where are you in the story now?

2. **Failure Woes.** Bring to mind a current or recent time of discouragement due to a feeling of failure. Which of the failure woes did you experience? Did you find yourself out of it? How?

3. **Learn Lessons, Lose Count.** What failures have you "learned" from? What failures might you need to lose count of? What makes the difference?

4. **But First, Rest.** What new insights did you develop on rest and sleep? How will you integrate these insights moving forward?

5. **Revisit the Goals, Refresh the Vision.** What is your vision? What goals do you have now that currently support your vision? Might there be a goal that you can expand or change that helps refresh your vision?

6. **Reframe Failure as Opportunity.** "When 'failure' meets you at your doorstep, pick it up, take it in, and put it in a different frame. Change the story." How does this land for you? What current or recent "failure" in your life needs to be put in a different frame? What opportunity have you just been presented with?

CHAPTER 6—ANXIETY: OUR NEED TO FEEL SAFE

1. **Anxiety Defined.** "Anxiety is what we feel when we don't feel safe." Is this a new or familiar definition of anxiety for you? Is it helpful? Discuss.

2. **The Anxiety Spectrum.** Is this a new way of looking at anxiety for you? Is it helpful? Discuss.

3. **High-Functioning Anxiety.** Do you or someone you know struggle with high-functioning anxiety? Discuss what it has looked and felt like.

4. **A Less Classic Theory: A Shift in Values.** Do you see a link between the shift in our culture's values and anxiety? Do you see a connection between these in your own anxiety journey?

5. **The Wisdom of Anxiety.** Of the three questions you can ask yourself about your anxiety—Am I in danger? What are my

current thoughts? Is there anything unresolved within me?—which ones bring you the most clarity and understanding about your own anxiety? Discuss.

6. **A Relieving Regimen.** Of the three anxiety-relieving methods discussed in this section—deep breathing, imagery, and meditation—which ones have you tried and found helpful? Which ones are you willing to try? How would you know they are helping?

CHAPTER 7—SADNESS AND DEPRESSION: OUR NEED FOR HEALTHY THINKING, CONNECTION, AND MEANING

1. **Making Room for Sadness.** How comfortable are you making room for sadness? Where do your thoughts and beliefs about dealing with sadness come from?

2. **A Note on Suicide: the Reality and the Myths.** How did these myths land for you? Are there any that surprised you? Where have your beliefs about depression and suicide come from?

3. **Broken Thinking, Broken Brain.** What new insights did you develop about the role of thinking and the brain in depression? Is this helpful for you? Discuss.

4. **Psalm 77.** As you reflect on Psalm 77, what do you sense God is trying to tell you? How do these words speak into your journey through depression?

5. **Loneliness and Disconnection.** What matters to you, and who are you sharing it with? How deep are your current connections?

6. **Loss of Meaning.** Are you experiencing purpose, moral value, self-efficacy, and positive self-worth in your life right now? If so, how? If not, what steps can you take to create more meaning in your life?

CHAPTER 8—ENVY: OUR NEED FOR ENOUGHNESS

1. **Not All Envy Is Created Equal.** What types of things have made you feel envy? Can you think of instances where you have felt malicious envy? Can you think of instances where you have felt benign envy?

2. **Our Need for Enoughness.** Discuss your journey with worthiness and enoughness. Have you ever been motivated by a need to prove your worth? Where did this need come from? How would you know if this need was motivating you now?

3. **What Are You *Really* Missing?** Think about a time you felt envy. What was the deep need behind the feeling?

4. **The Thing About Comparison.** What new insights did you gain about comparison? What might be helpful in your journey through comparison and envy?

5. **Social Media: Fanning Flames of Envy.** What do you need to change about your social media patterns or regimen to better honor yourself? What other ways in real life can you get your needs met?

6. **God Chose the Weak Things of the World.** What does 1 Corinthians 1:27-29 mean for you? Are there any insights in these verses that speak to your journey through envy?

CHAPTER 9—SHAME: OUR NEED FOR RADICAL LOVE

1. **Shame Undercover.** Of the six silent ways shame operates in our lives, which do you resonate with? How have you seen shame play out in your life?

2. **Healthy Shame Versus Guilt.** How have you understood shame and guilt? Does this chapter shed new light on your definitions? Would you add anything to these definitions?

3. **Healthy Shame Versus Toxic Shame.** Can you think of a time when you experienced healthy shame? Can you think of a time when you felt toxic shame? What motivated these experiences? What were the outcomes? What was the main difference?

4. **Unspoken Family Rules and Shame.** What unspoken rules do you recall from your family of origin? How have you seen these rules impact your experience of shame?

5. **Our Need for Radical Love.** "Radical love heals radical shame." How did this land for you? What does this mean to you? What would it look like for you to lean more into God's radical love for you?

6. **Seek Reparative Relationship.** Where in your life do you have reparative relationship? How can you strengthen it? If you are not in a reparative relationship, how will you begin to find or create one?

NOTES

INTRODUCTION: IT'S WHO WE ARE

[1]Chris Tomlin, "Good Good Father," by Tony Brown and Pat Barrett, track 1 on *Never Lose Sight*, sixstepsrecords, 2016.

1 THE DANGER OF SPIRITUAL BYPASSING

[1]Diana Raab, "What Is Spiritual Bypassing?" *Psychology Today*, January 13, 2019, www.psychologytoday.com/us/blog/the-empowerment-diary/201901/what-is-spiritual-bypassing.

[2]Beverley Fehr and James A. Russell, "Concept of Emotion Viewed from a Prototype Perspective," *Journal of Experimental Psychology* 113, no. 3 (1984): 464-86, https://pdfs.semanticscholar.org/4c25/97a92ce4de6b58e7c2b4140eed1c1046ffbd.pdf.

2 UNCOVERING OUR CORE BELIEFS

[1]Zachary Crockett, "How Rich Would You Be If You Actually Got a Penny for Every Thought?" *Vox*, December 6, 2016, www.vox.com/culture/2016/12/6/13821430/penny-every-thought-rich.

[2]John Piper, "Must Bible Reading Always End with an Application?" *Desiring God*, February 13, 2003, www.desiringgod.org/interviews/must-bible-reading-always-end-with-application.

[3]"Kardia," Bible Study Tools.com, www.biblestudytools.com/lexicons/greek/nas/kardia.html.

3 TRAUMA: OUR NEED TO TELL OUR STORY

[1]Sarah Montana, "The Real Risk of Forgiveness—and Why It's Worth It," talk given at TEDxLincolnSquare, March 2018, www.ted.com/talks/sarah_montana_why_forgiveness_is_worth_it?language=en.

4 HURT: OUR NEED TO RECOVER WHAT'S LOST

[1]Martin H. Teicher, Jacqueline A. Samson, Ann Polcari, and Cynthia E. Mc-Greenery, "Sticks, Stones, and Hurtful Words: Relative Effects of Various Forms of Childhood Maltreatment," *The American Journal of Psychiatry* 163, no. 6 (2006): 993-1000. DOI: 10.1176/ajp.2006.163.6.993.

[2]Martin H. Teicher, Jacqueline A. Samson, Yi-Shin Sheu, Ann Polcari, and Cynthia E. McGreenery, "Hurtful Words: Exposure to Peer Verbal Aggression Is Associated with Elevated Psychiatric Symptom Scores and Corpus Callosum Abnormalities," *The American Journal of Psychiatry* 167, no. 12 (2010): 1464-71, https://doi.org/10.1176/appi.ajp.2010.10010030.

[3]Christina Hibbert, "Self-Esteem vs. Self-Worth: Q&A with Dr. Christina Hibbert," DrChristinaHibbert.com, March 9, 2014, www.drchristinahibbert.com/self-esteem-vs-self-worth.

[4]Helen Fisher, "Lust, Attraction, and Attachment in Mammalian Reproduction," *Human Nature* 9, no. 1 (1998): 23-52, https://doi.org/10.1007/s12110-998-1010-5.

[5]Nathan DeWall, Geoff MacDonald, Gregory D. Webster, et al., "Acetaminophen Reduces Social Pain: Behavioral and Neural Evidence," *Psychological Science* 21, no. 7 (2010): 931-37, https://doi.org/10.1177/0956797610374741.

5 DISCOURAGEMENT: OUR NEED FOR CONFIDENCE AND COURAGE

[1]Kylie Blenkhorn, "Infertility: It's Real and It Hurts," HuffPost.com, August 3, 2016, www.huffpost.com/entry/infertility-its-real-and-it-hurts_b_577c2feee4b00a3ae4ce7692.

[2]"How Common Is Infertility? Your Guide," *The Fertility Institute Blog*, The Fertility Institute, updated March 22, 2020, https://fertilityinstitute.com/is-infertility-common/.

[3]Ian H. Robertson, *The Winner Effect: The Neuroscience of Success and Failure* (New York: Thomas Dunne Books, 2012).

[4]Ian Robertson, quoted by Joshua A. Krisch, "The Winner Effect: Why Alpha Males (and Mice) Keep on Winning," Fatherly, July 19, 2017, www.fatherly.com/health-science/winner-effect/.

6 ANXIETY: OUR NEED TO FEEL SAFE

[1]Christopher Ingraham, "America's Top Fears: Public Speaking, Heights, and Bugs," *Washington Post*, October 30, 2014, www.washingtonpost.com/news/wonk/wp/2014/10/30/clowns-are-twice-as-scary-to-democrats-as-they-are-to-republicans.

[2]"Majority of Americans Say They Are Anxious About Health; Millennials Are More Anxious Than Baby Boomers," American Psychiatric Association news release, May 22, 2017, www.psychiatry.org/newsroom/news-releases/majority-of-americans-say-they-are-anxious-about-health-millennials-are-more-anxious-than-baby-boomers.

[3]Tim Kasser and Richard M. Ryan, "Further Examining the American Dream: Differential Correlates of Intrinsic and Extrinsic Goals," *Personality and Social Psychology Bulletin* 22, no. 3 (1996): 280-87, https://doi.org/10.1177/01461672962 23006.

[4]Tim Kasser, "What Psychology Says About Materialism and the Holidays," American Psychological Association, December 16, 2014, www.apa.org/news /press/releases/2014/12/materialism-holidays.

[5]Angela Neal-Barnett, *Soothe Your Nerves: The Black Woman's Guide to Understanding and Overcoming Anxiety, Panic, and Fearz* (New York: Simon & Schuster, 2003).

[6]"Meditation," PsychologyToday.com, www.psychologytoday.com/us/basics /meditation.

7 SADNESS AND DEPRESSION: OUR NEED FOR HEALTHY THINKING, CONNECTION, AND MEANING

[1]Elisabeth Kübler-Ross and David Kessler, *On Grief and Grieving: Finding the Meaning of Grief Through the Five Stages of Loss* (New York: Scriber, 2004).

[2]Ronnie Janoff-Bulman, *Shattered Assumptions: Towards a New Psychology of Trauma* (New York: Free Press, 1992).

[3]Caroline Leaf, *Switch On Your Brain: The Key to Peak Happiness, Thinking, and Health* (Grand Rapids: Baker Books, 2015).

[4]Quoted in Johann Hari, *Lost Connections: Uncovering the Real Causes of Depression—and the Unexpected Solutions* (New York: Bloomsbury USA, 2018).

[5]"Loneliness Is at Epidemic Levels in America," Cigna press release, January 23, 2020, www.cigna.com/about-us/newsroom/studies-and-reports/combatting -loneliness.

[6]John Cacioppo, "Loneliness Within a Nomological Net: An Evolutionary Perspective," *Journal of Research in Personality* 40, no. 6 (2006), https://doi .org/10.1016/j.jrp.2005.11.007.

[7]Clay Routledge, "Suicides Have Increased. Is This an Existential Crisis?" *New York Times*, June 23, 2018, www.nytimes.com/2018/06/23/opinion/sunday/suicide -rate-existential-crisis.html.

[8]Stephen Ilardi, *The Depression Cure: The 6-Step Program to Beat Depression Without Drugs* (Cambridge, MA: Da Capo Press, 2009).

[9]Thane M. Erickson et al., "Compassionate and Self-Image Goals as Interpersonal Maintenance Factors in Clinical Depression and Anxiety," *Journal of Clinical Psychology* 74, no. 4 (September 12, 2017): 608-625, https://doi.org/10.1002 /jclp.22524.

8 ENVY: OUR NEED FOR ENOUGHNESS

[1]Nicole E. Henniger and Christine R. Harris, "Envy Across Adulthood: The What and the Who," *Basic and Applied Social Psychology* 37, no. 6 (2015).

[2]Quoted in Bertrand Russell, *The Conquest of Happiness* (New York: Liveright Publishing Corp., 2013).

[3]Richard H. Smith, "The Important Distinction Between Benign and Malicious Envy," *Psychology Today,* July 11, 2015, www.psychologytoday.com/us/blog/joy -and-pain/201501/the-important-distinction-between-benign-and-malicious -envy.

[4]Richard H. Smith, ed., *Envy: Theory and Research,* Series in Affective Science (Oxford: Oxford University Press, 2008).

[5]Rachel Andrew, quoted by Moya Sarner, "The Age of Envy: How to Be Happy When Everyone Else's Life Looks Perfect," *The Guardian*, October 9, 2018, www .theguardian.com/lifeandstyle/2018/oct/09/age-envy-be-happy-everyone -else-perfect-social-media.

9 SHAME: OUR NEED FOR RADICAL LOVE

[1]Joseph Burgo, "The Difference Between Guilt and Shame," *Psychology Today* blog, May 30, 2103, www.psychologytoday.com/us/blog/shame/201305/the -difference-between-guilt-and-shame.

ABOUT THE AUTHOR

E QUIPPED WITH A BA in psychology from UCLA and a master's and doctorate in psychology from Azusa Pacific University, Dr. Peace Amadi is a psychology professor, speaker, children's book author, content creator, and host. As a woman of faith, she uses her various platforms to bridge the gap between mental health and faith for the purposes of engaging a deeper healing journey. As a woman of Nigerian descent, she calls for reflection on how healing is impacted also by culture. In her personal time, she enjoys creating meaningful moments with friends and family, drinking sweet iced coffees, and digging up stories she'll find some new way to share.

You can stay connected with her at
@itspeaceamadi on Instagram and Twitter.